You Got Style

You Got Style

HOW DISCOVERING YOUR PERSONAL
STYLE IMPACTS YOUR FAITH, FAMILY,
FINANCES, AND MUCH MORE

Rick McDaniel

CrossLink Publishing
RAPID CITY, SD

McDaniel/CrossLink Publishing
1601 Mt. Rushmore Rd., Ste 3288
Rapid City, SD 57701
www.CrossLinkPublishing.com

Ordering Information:
Quantity sales. Special discounts are available on quantity purchases by corporations, associations, and others. For details, contact the "Special Sales Department" at the address above.

You Got Style/ McDaniel —1st ed.
ISBN 978-1-63357-178-5
Library of Congress Control Number: 2019939182

Cover Design by Matt McGhan.

To the people of Richmond Community Church:

Experiencing your many and varied styles over the last twenty-five years has enriched my life tremendously.

Contents

INTRODUCTION

When you hear the word *style*, you usually think of fashion. People may choose to wear clothes that are preppy, tailored, casual, or even unusual. What we wear communicates our personal style. But there is much more to our style than the clothes we wear. Different people look at situations differently. God created us with different personalities, different cultures, different ethnicities, different genders, and different backgrounds. These distinctions influence our opinions and behaviors about many things and produce a variety of styles.

Discovering your individual style can help you understand why you do certain things, why you react in a particular way to something, and why others act the way they do. These styles involve the most important aspects of our lives, including our relationships, our family, our faith, our finances and our work. We are all different, and we all have different styles.

I started studying styles more than fifteen years ago. I was doing research for a message entitled "Till Debt Do Us Part." I knew that conflict over money was the greatest source of arguments between married couples, and I wanted to help the couples in my church. I read an article on different financial styles, and it formed the basis for my message that week.

As I continued to research and study, I discovered many more styles. And over the years I spoke on giving styles, faith styles, spiritual styles, time styles, and decision styles. Each time I spoke about styles, I would hear from many people about how helpful the information was to them.

I became attuned to anything I read that might be about style. As I studied them further, I began to categorize the numerous unique styles. Around four years ago I came to realize this information could help so many more people, so I began writing about each individual style.

This book explores the styles that I believe impact our lives the most. Each chapter explains a given style and how a person may exhibit that style. And since Jesus has impacted more lives than any other person in history, I've devoted the last chapter to the style of Jesus.

Learning about your style and the styles of others can increase happiness, bring greater understanding, generate success, and reduce conflict in our lives and the lives of those around us.

Our interest in learning more about ourselves is obvious. The huge popularity of online personality quizzes proves it. It isn't surprising, given our age-old fascination with the central question, "Who am I?" Now combine that with our interest in comparing ourselves to others in our social media-obsessed culture.

Personality quizzes have been around for decades, especially in magazines for women and teens. Online quizzes can be found on sites like Zimbio.com, amongst others. But the greatest prevalence is on Facebook with quizzes developed by BuzzFeed.com. This website has pumped out a multitude of quizzes, the most popular being "Which State Do You Actually Come From?"

Beyond the online quizzes are a variety of personality assessments that are often utilized by employers and job seekers. These provide a great means for self-knowledge. They highlight ways of thinking and patterns of behavior. They guide us to a better understanding of ourselves and can help us create positive change in our lives. The Myers-Briggs Type Indicator and the DISC assessment are some well-known personality tests.

All of these self-discovery tools are valuable, but *You Got Style* is unique. In this book I explain how styles can impact virtually every aspect of your life. By the end of this book, you will

- Understand different financial styles and time styles that can enhance your marriage.

- Identify parenting styles and decision styles to benefit every family.

- Discover work styles and leadership styles that can bring you greater success in your career.

- Discern spiritual styles and faith styles to enrich your spiritual life.

- Understand thinking styles and learning styles that will help you maximize your intellect.

- Recognize retirement styles and giving styles to make you happier.

- Learn about the styles of Jesus and how modeling them can change your life forever.

So, let's go discover your unique styles!

CHAPTER ONE

FINANCIAL STYLES

We have all heard these phrases many times: Money makes the world go 'round. Money talks. Show me the money. Money is a big deal to just about everyone. We want it, fight about it, and worry about it. Making money, spending money, and saving money are topics about which volumes have been written. The economy is a daily discussion in the media, politics, and business. TV networks and publications of every kind are exclusively focused on money. Entire careers are dedicated to managing and investing money. There is the Dow-Jones Industrial Average, the NASDAQ, and the various commodity markets. There are interest rates, Treasury bills, and mutual funds. No one can ignore the impact of money on our world today.

The Bible has much to say about money. In fact there are 2,285 verses (1 out of every 6 verses in the New Testament) about money, more than on hope (185), faith (246), and even love (733)—the defining message of Jesus! For there to be so many more verses on money, God must have known money would be a challenge for us, and that's why he gave us a great amount of instruction about it. Sixteen of the thirty-eight parables of Jesus are about money and wealth. Parables were Jesus's signature way of communicating truth. If almost half of all the parables are about money, then Jesus wants us to understand it well. Jesus said, "You cannot serve both God and money" (Matthew 6:24). He knew money could dominate our thinking and cause us great anxiety. And in one of the most misinterpreted scriptures in the Bible, I Timothy 6:10, tells us, "The love of money causes all kinds of trouble." It's not saying money is evil or that money is the cause of every trouble. Other popular Bible translations (like the King James Version and New International Version) call money "the root of all evil," but this just communicates that money will create many problems for us.

Survey after survey says the number one reason for conflict in a marriage is finances. As a pastor, I totally concur with the research. Money as a source of conflict can be easily understood if we realize a simple truth: People have different financial styles. Understanding your style and that of your spouse will not automatically solve any financial conflict, but it will help you speak to each other in a way that acknowledges your innate differences. Even if you are not married, you still need to understand your financial style and the style of your loved ones who impact your life in a financial way.

Roper/Starch Worldwide is a market research firm who did a study for *Worth* magazine about Americans' use of money (Sullivan 1994). They talked to 2,000 people across America, asking them eighty-three questions about how they make, spend, and think about money. Their survey provides a valuable financial insight into the habits, priorities, and personalities of Americans. They discovered that America is evenly split between those who think money can buy happiness and those who don't. But most Americans would rather be richer than smarter, thinner, or better looking.

The most fascinating information to come out of the Roper/Starch survey was the identification of seven distinct financial personalities, which I refer to as financial styles. Beyond these seven is the style the Bible teaches every Christ follower to have in regard to money. How are we to earn, spend, invest, and give money in a way that pleases Jesus? We will identify that style, but first we will examine each of the initial seven financial styles.

Idealist

The idealist's motto is, "There's more to life than money." These folks are almost indifferent to money. They have the second-lowest mean income and are fine making do with less. Most believe that doubling their income would not make them happier. The idealist sees money as nothing more than security, but it is not something to be relied upon or trusted in. A vast majority believe money is the root of all evil (even though that is misquoting the Bible verse) and that money means nothing without someone to share it with.

People with this style do not link money to happiness. They do not believe a happy marriage depends upon sharing a similar economic background, that the spouse who makes the most money should have more power, or that there comes a point in a marriage where money is more important than romance. Money and material things are simply not that important.

Idealists do not get emotionally involved in making or losing money. Most would only be a little upset if they lost a lot of money in the stock market. But they are not likely to put a lot of money in the stock market since so few own any stocks. If they make an investment, it's usually a modest one. If this style fits you, you likely perceive money as simply a necessity in life—nothing more, nothing less.

Hunter

The hunter's motto is, "Nothing ventured, nothing gained." Hunters earn the highest income of all the styles. They are aggressive about making, spending, and investing money. Hunters look to optimize their financial resources at every opportunity. They desire money and equate it with success, power, and happiness. Most are comfortable talking about money and how much they have.

Hunters are confident in their ability to make money. They believe in taking financial risks in order to get ahead. Most feel more comfortable about choosing investments than the rest of us. More than any other financial style, hunters believe their intelligence and courage are keys to financial success. Their aggressive nature leads to turbulent personal lives. They will win arguments about money with their spouse but are unlikely to resolve conflict about romance. Hunters have the second-highest divorce rate among all the styles.

Hunters want to do something with their money. The idea of a low-interest bearing savings account or CD (certificate of deposit) is underwhelming to them. They look for new investment opportunities and are comfortable with a higher level of risk. Even if they lose money, they feel they are wiser the next time they invest. Hunters worry about things they cannot control but they don't worry about money. If this style fits you, money is probably something you are comfortable with and want to continue to make more of.

Striver

The striver's motto is, "Money makes the world go 'round." This style, more than any other, is controlled by money. They have the lowest income of any financial style, and they are twice as likely as the average person to think of money as bringing power or happiness. Most strivers believe no one can have too much money.

A majority of strivers have not attended college, and their lack of education puts them at a financial disadvantage. Few consider themselves well-informed on financial matters. Yet, few will ever be happy making only an average amount of money. For strivers, most household issues stem from money and who controls it. Not surprisingly, strivers are the most likely of any style to be divorced.

Strivers are jealous of people who have wealth. Most believe wealth makes people more attractive than they would otherwise be. They also assume people who have money didn't earn it but simply had the right connections or were fortunate to have been born with wealth. They see themselves as poor with little opportunity for change.

They do not save, and they spend what little they have. If you fit this style, your relationship with money is most likely very strained.

Nester

The nester's motto is, "Happiness is having just enough to get by." Nesters are the least engaged of all styles with their financial lives. They are not financially savvy or tied up emotionally with their money. Their financial concerns are focused primarily on themselves and their families. They have a pragmatic view of money—it fulfills their immediate needs.

Nesters do not want a lot of money but interestingly what they have they see as theirs alone. Few see themselves leaving money for their heirs, and most nesters believe individuals should look out for themselves when it comes to money. They do not think extravagantly because they will most likely not act on their extravagant desires. Monthly bills are the focus much more than growing their wealth through investments.

Nesters are the least likely of any style to make getting ahead financially a top priority and the least likely to agree that the size of their bank account speaks to who they are. They are also the least likely to agree that a person can never be too rich. Nesters simply refuse to be defined by how much money they have. If you fit this style, being comfortable is probably all you really want from your wealth.

Splurger

The splurger's motto is, "It's more blessed to receive." They are average in terms of their income, but that does not stop them from spending. They are the most self-indulgent of the financial styles. When given the option, splurgers are three times more likely than everyone else to buy a luxury item instead of a practical one, whether they can afford it or not. Their top money priority is financial independence, but they are so averse to risk that most of their investments are in CDs and savings accounts. A majority of splurgers expect to be better off financially five years from now.

The splurger is like the hunter but without the financial acumen. They don't want to just accumulate money—they want to spend it. Splurgers are somewhat impractical in that they spend like someone with far greater wealth. They tend to be self-centered and are the most likely of all the styles to disagree with Acts 20:35 (NLT): "It is more blessed to give than to receive."

Splurgers are apt to buy really nice things regardless of whether they need them, and they identify themselves as being indulgent rather than practical. They are also twice as likely to be impressed with someone who purchases only the best of everything. If you fit this style, you probably see money as simply a means to consumption.

Protector

The protector's motto is, "It's more blessed to give than to receive." Protectors are the second most financially savvy style, but they view money differently. They are much more likely to be concerned about other people. Money is a means for helping children, parents, and friends. A majority of protectors think it is right to consider other people before themselves in financial matters. They do not think of money in terms of power but security.

Protectors are primarily women, and they tend to be college educated. Of all the financial styles, they are most likely to be married and the least likely to be divorced. They are the second highest in income and have a higher percentage of volunteerism. Getting ahead financially is simply not a top priority. Money is a means to provide security for their families.

Protectors are not very interested in purchasing items for themselves. They almost feel guilty spending money on themselves when there are others to buy for. They would rather use their money so family or friends can receive a gift. Protectors do not equate self-worth with financial success. They are among the least likely to see work as anything more than a way to make money. If you fit this style, you likely see money as something to be used to do good.

Gatherer

The gatherer's motto is, "Better safe than sorry." Gatherers tend to be conservative and modest, and they consider themselves to be disciplined spenders and competent in financial matters. They feel the most confident of any financial style when it comes to making a major purchase (like a new car), financing or refinancing a house, or filing an insurance claim.

They look out for themselves first when it comes to finances. Gatherers are often tight with what they consider their hard-earned money. They are comfortable with managing money, understand how money works, and use it how they deem best. They are the typical conservative American investor. Gatherers are more likely to own stocks or bonds than the average person—specifically, they are more likely than any other financial style to have three or more investments. They are not gamblers; money is simply security for them.

Maybe most telling is that a majority of gatherers agree that it is more important to plan for the future than to enjoy what I have now." Though they value their money, gatherers do believe it is wrong to desire money too much. In fact, more than any other style, they are satisfied with their paycheck. If you fit this style, you probably see money as something you are comfortable with and need to take care of for the future.

Steward

This is the financial style that the Bible teaches. *Steward* is an old word that needs a modern understanding. The original Greek word in the New Testament comes from the root word for "house" or "household" (*oikos*). The steward was the "householder" (*oikonomos*)—the person responsible for running the household. The role originated in ancient times when wealthy property owners would appoint a steward to handle their household affairs when they went out of town. The steward would run the entire household business as if it were his own. The best modern term for this ancient concept is "manager." Thus, financial stewards manage money as though it's theirs even though it's really not.

The steward's motto is, "Where your treasure is, there your heart will be also" (Matthew 6:21 NIV). This is another of the most misquoted scriptures in the Bible. Most people think the Bible teaches that where your heart is, that is where your treasure will be, but this is not the case. Rather, your heart will always be where your treasure is. Stewards understand two basic concepts: everything belongs to God (Psalm 24:1), and they are to be faithful with what God has given them (Luke 12:42, I Corinthians 4:2).

Stewards resemble idealists in that they do not focus on money, but they are much more financially savvy. They have a sensible and sound understanding of money. Stewards are the least anxious about money of any style. Unlike hunters, they do not look to money as their source of power, security, or happiness. They trust God to provide for them and take care of their needs. Stewards work hard, but unlike gatherers, they realize that what they have is the result of God's provision rather than their own labor. They are wise in making purchases and are not extravagant. Unlike splurgers, they are not driven to buy status items or pleasure purchases. They are guided by need and budget more than fad or fashion.

Stewards may not be aggressive investors but they are productive ones. Unlike nesters, they are savers and investors because they realize it is actually God's money they are managing. They look for ways to invest money that will bring a good return. They understand consistent saving and wise investing. Stewards believe in wise money management, so they live by a budget and try to be debt free. Unlike the striver, they recognize that money is not the most important thing in life. They put their relationship with God and their family before financial matters.

The defining characteristic of a steward is their generosity. They do not cling to their possessions or fixate on their money. Stewards know that giving draws them closer to God because God is a giver. They know giving is the one guaranteed way to break the grip of materialism in their lives. Stewards know they will live a blessed and happy life because you can't out-give God. They put God first in every area of life, and that certainly includes their finances. Stewards are faithful to support God's kingdom with their financial resources. They are channels of God's blessings, not reservoirs. Supporting the work of the church and helping those in need are their top priorities. Stewards realize life on earth is brief and that they have an eternal perspective. They know their giving is actually making eternal investments where a return is guaranteed.

· · · · ·

Money is essential for life, and understanding your financial style is very helpful. But fixating on money can take you away from what God wants for your life. If you are not careful, your stuff can end up owning you instead of you owning it. Relationships can be destroyed over money, and far too many marriages have fallen apart because of it. No matter your financial style, it is a fallacy to think money can solve every problem. Money can bring a level of security, a certain amount of happiness, and a degree of power. But it can so easily cause us to confuse our priorities. When we worry about money, it shows a lack of trust in God. The power of money is crystal clear, and the more we can do to understand how we relate to it, the better.

FINANCIAL STYLES INVENTORY

- For each statement, mark to what extent it is true of your life:

  3=VERY

  2=SOME

  1=LITTLE

  0=NOT AT ALL

  Put a number in the blank before each statement.

- Transfer the numbers you gave for each statement to the grid at the end of the inventory.

- Total each column. The highest number identifies your preferred financial style; the next highest number, your secondary style.

☐ 1. I am not comfortable in my ability to choose a sound investment.

☐ 2. I believe in taking financial risks to get ahead.

☐ 3. I believe wealth makes a person more attractive.

☐ 4. I am at a loss about assessing my options when it comes to buying life insurance.

☐ 5. I most enjoy buying luxury items whether I can afford it or not.

☐ 6. Money is more about security than power.

☐ 7. When it comes to money, a person has to look out for themselves first.

☐ 8. I see money as security and not something to be relied upon or trusted in.

☐ 9. Money is something I am comfortable with and want to make more of.

☐ 10. I don't think there is any such thing as too much money.

☐ 11. I feel it is more important to enjoy what I have now than to plan for the future.

☐ 12. Financial independence is my top priority.

☐ 13. I feel quite competent about assessing my options when choosing a sound investment.

☐ 14. I am confident about making a major purchase, like a new car, financing or refinancing a house, or filing an insurance claim.

☐ 15. I believe money is the root of all evil.

☐ 16. I believe my intelligence and courage are keys to financial success.

☐ 17. I am jealous of people who have wealth.

☐ 18. Financially, I like to focus on myself and my family first.

☐ 19. I don't like to take risks with my investments.

☐ 20. In financial matters, it is more important to think of others than myself.

☐ 21. I am comfortable managing money and know how money works.

☐ 22. To me money means nothing without someone to share it with.

☐ 23. I do not worry about money.

☐ 24. I think financial success is determined by luck or connections.

☐ 25. I am more concerned with paying the monthly bills than making investments.

☐ 26. I would rather spend my money than save it for a rainy day.

☐ 27. I feel guilty about spending money on myself.

☐ 28. Since money means security to me, I don't like to gamble it away.

☐ 29. I think money is a necessity, nothing more and nothing less.

☐ 30. I am aggressive about making, spending and investing money.

☐ 31. I like to spend what I have rather than save.

☐ 32. I believe being comfortable financially is more important than being wealthy.

☐ 33. I believe I will be better off financially five years from now.

☐ 34. I think money is something to be used to do good.

☐ 35. I believe it is more important to plan for the future than to enjoy what I have now.

☐ 36. My financial motto is "There's more to life than money."

☐ 37. My financial motto is "Nothing ventured, nothing gained."

☐ 38. My financial motto is "Money makes the world go 'round."

☐ 39. My financial motto is "Happiness is having just enough to get by."

☐ 40. My financial motto is "It is more blessed to receive."

☐ 41. My financial motto is "It's more blessed to give than to receive."

☐ 42. My financial motto is "Better safe than sorry."

1.	2.	3.	4.	5.	6.	7.
8.	9.	10.	11.	12.	13.	14.
15.	16.	17.	18.	19.	20.	21
22.	23.	24.	25.	26.	27.	28.
29.	30.	31.	32.	33.	34.	35.
36.	37.	8.	39.	40.	41.	42.
Total	Total	Total	Total	Total	Total	Total
Idealistic	Hunter	Striver	Nester	Splurger	Protector	Gatherer

CHAPTER TWO

SPIRITUAL STYLES

You can take a giant step forward in your spiritual growth and relationship with God by syncing up with the natural way in which you connect with God. While there is only one way to God, through Jesus Christ, there are many ways to connect with God and get to Jesus—many different spiritual styles.

A spiritual style is the way that you relate to God. It's how you connect with him. And that style is unique to you. If you don't identify your spiritual style, then it is difficult to experience God's presence in your everyday life. You may have some understanding of your spiritual style, but this chapter will help you gain an even greater understanding of it. If you've struggled to connect with God in a meaningful way, learning your spiritual style will result in a more vibrant spiritual life.

Most people have a predominate and secondary spiritual style, just like they have predominate and secondary personality traits. Gary Thomas wrote a book called *Sacred Pathways: Discover Your Soul's Path to God*, and much of the information I provide in this chapter is based on that book (Thomas 1996). John Ortberg and others have also written about the different spiritual pathways to God. I'm calling them spiritual styles. And I'm going to identify the ones that I believe are appropriate for a person who is seeking to know God more.

Naturalist

The naturalist is the person who connects with God through nature—on a mountain, in the woods, by a river, etc. This is when they sense God's presence, and nature replenishes them spiritually. They feel energized by God when they are in that natural setting. They consider the greatness and vastness of creation—mountains and valleys, rivers and streams, deserts and forests. They marvel at how the Rockies are different from the White Mountains, which are different from the Appalachians, which are different from the deserts, which are different from the rain forests, which are different from the beaches.

Being around nature helps the naturalist see the multitude of God's beauty and creation, and that helps them connect with God. The naturalist believes that nature proclaims and reveals who God is. So whether they're watching a butterfly or ocean waves crashing into rocks, that is more spiritually meaningful to the naturalist than listening to a sermon or reading a book. The naturalist can visualize spiritual truth and sees the physical as mirroring the spiritual. The unseen spiritual world becomes more real to them when they get in touch with the physical, natural world.

Within the Bible, John the Baptist would have been a naturalist. Dr. Paul Brand would have also been a naturalist, and Gary Thomas, who wrote *Sacred Pathways*, identifies himself as a naturalist. If you're a naturalist, you probably consider taking a walk in the woods or hiking up a mountain to be a spiritual experience, not just physical exercise. Though others may not understand a naturalist's motivation to hike a mountain, you know that it's a way to draw closer to God. That's your spiritual style.

Intellectual

Individuals with an intellectual spiritual style need their mind activated in order to connect with God. Intellectuals enjoy studying and discussing the Bible, theology, church history, apologetics (how one defends the Christian faith), and hermeneutics (how to correctly interpret the Bible). The more they learn about God, the closer they get to God.

The intellectual wants to think more than they want to feel about their faith. It's not that they're unfeeling or lack feelings, but they want to come to God through their mind. Faith to them is something to be understood as much as it is to be experienced. Some people criticize this mentality by saying, "You need to get in touch with your feelings and emotions in order to experience God." And an intellectual person can rightfully respond, "No. First and foremost, I need to connect with God through my mind, because that's the kind of spiritual style I have. That's the pathway that leads me to connecting with God and growing with him."

The apostle Paul is a great biblical example of this style, and C.S. Lewis and Chuck Colson are marvelous contemporary examples of intellectuals. These are people who came to God through intellect and who wanted other people to understand that they could come to God through their mind too. If this is your spiritual style, this might be a freeing moment for you, realizing that it's okay to use your brain and enjoy studying things.

Contemplative

The contemplative person connects with God through uninterrupted time alone with him. The key word is *alone*. Contemplative individuals are sometimes criticized about their social habits. "Why don't you like to be around people more? Why aren't you in this particular group?" Contemplative people simply prioritize their time alone with God. They have a large capacity for prayer and can often pray much longer than others. That doesn't make them better or more spiritual. This is just their spiritual style. They value solitude and simplicity.

The contemplative usually lives a simple life that's not very materialistic. They want the spiritual focus to be on being more than doing or acquiring more. However, this doesn't mean that doing things for God is inappropriate or should be discouraged. Contemplative individuals are just more introspective and internally focused.

A contemplative does not like a lot of outward distractions, and as a result, they may find themselves at odds with those who have other spiritual styles that are inherently distracting. Contemplative individuals often engage in meditation and centering prayer, which is prayer that centers on just one word or phrase that's repeated over and over again. They like to incorporate "the Jesus Prayer" into centered prayer sessions because it's short and easy to repeat. These are the kind of folks who really like to do kind things for others secretly or anonymously. They may secretly bless someone, secretly pray for someone, or secretly give something to someone.

Within the Bible, Mary, Martha's sister, is a prime example of a contemplative person. She just wanted to be with Jesus, while Martha wanted to do things for Jesus. Richard Foster is a contemplative who wrote *Celebration of Discipline*, which I highly recommend. He also wrote *Prayer*, another great book. Dallas Willard is another example of someone who embodies this spiritual style. Historically there have been many, many contemplatives throughout church history, such as Brother Lawrence and Teresa of Avila.

Activist

The activist connects with God through action. They are a single-minded, focused person who has a strong sense of vision that guides them spiritually. They have great passion—for the church, for expanding and growing the kingdom, and for justice. They want to right wrongs and call things out that are sinful or evil.

Activists interact with people, confront them, take risks, and strive to bring out the God-given potential of others. They seek to make a difference with their faith. When they see change, when they see growth, when they see impact, they connect with God in a greater way.

Activists really want to take on causes they feel are just and right. Nehemiah was a biblical activist. He saw the need for the walls of Jerusalem to be rebuilt, so he took on the job of rebuilding them. William Booth, who founded the Salvation Army, was an activist. And in more modern times, Bill Hybels, my mentor, is a great example of an activist; he started a whole new movement of churches—the contemporary seeker-church movement. Activists connect with God through doing things for God and others.

Traditionalist

The traditionalist connects with God through ritual and liturgy. These individuals really love and are moved by symbols and icons, such as crosses. They are the people who are eager to practice the sacraments that really define historic Christian faith. They want to be traditional in the truest sense of that word. They want to go all the way back to the apostles and try to follow their ancient traditions.

The folks who like to follow the Christian calendar are often traditionalists. They want to observe the Epiphany, Lent, Easter, and Pentecost because they are traditions that they enjoy, even though some are not necessarily in the Bible. They like to repeat formal prayers that were written many years ago.

The traditionalists believe in a disciplined life of faith—that it is very important not just to attend church but to be a member. They consider things like prayer and tithing to be nonnegotiable. The Roman Catholic, Greek Orthodox, and Anglicans denominations often appeal to traditionalists because these groups embrace the long arc of Christian tradition.

Ezra was this kind of person in the Bible who was concerned with spiritual traditions and regulations. Someone like a Michael Youssef, who pastors a formal church in Atlanta, is an example of a modern traditionalist, even though he has a television broadcast ministry. D. James Kennedy and Mel Gibson are also traditionalists, even though Mel is a Hollywood movie star.

Enthusiast

The enthusiast connects with God through praise and worship. These are the people who say, "I'm about to get my praise on!" They really like the singing, worshiping, and celebratory aspects of praise.

Unlike intellectuals, who seek to engage their mind and don't care so much about feelings, enthusiasts don't care so much about the mind but definitely want to connect emotively. They want to feel God. And they love to worship and praise him. It's in the midst of worship that their heart comes alive and they feel close to God—when they are praising, rejoicing, and clapping. They love to feel moved by God and say things like, "The Spirit is alive and working." It doesn't mean that others don't believe the Spirit is alive and working. Being very vocal about praise and worship is just part of an enthusiast's spiritual style.

They are creative people, and thank God for them because they bring a lot of their creativity into the church. Unlike the contemplative, who often wants to be alone, they are highly relational and want to be around people: "When's the next time we can get together? What group can I go to?" They want to be wherever people are. They are also somewhat mystical and see things in a highly spiritual way. Enthusiasts really want other people to worship together and see what God might do in their midst.

King David was an enthusiast in the Bible. He loved to worship God and dance before him, despite his own wife's embarrassment at his display of emotion. Pastor Jack Hayford in California many years ago really started to write and proclaim a theology of worship, establishing himself as an enthusiast. And certainly someone like Chris Tomlin, who leads (in conjunction with others) the praise and worship movement, would also be an enthusiast.

Sensate

Sensate people connect with God through beauty and awe-inspiring sensory experiences. That's why they desire to be filled with sights, sounds, and smells. They need their senses to be activated in order to feel close to God. Some are moved spiritually by religious art. Others may view the same religious art and feel nothing, but for the sensate, the art connects them with God.

One of the greatest collections of religious art in the world is at the Rijksmuseum in Amsterdam. I've been there twice, and the collection is unbelievable. It includes many kinds of artwork created by some of the greatest artists of history that portray various biblical scenes or project a spiritual message.

A sensate would feel so close to God in such a place. They might also be moved by church architecture, like that of Duke Chapel at my alma mater, Duke University. It's one of the great examples in America of gothic architecture. Being a young country, we don't have a lot of historic cathedrals like Europe does. A sensate would walk into a place like Duke Chapel and be so moved by the stained glass, sculptures, and carvings. They would feel like they could really worship God better in that environment.

Sensates often enjoy classical music, especially compositions that are religiously inspired. They love to celebrate communion because the ritual puts them in touch with their senses when they touch the bread and drink the juice. It's something for them that's visual as well.

Sensates like to smell the incense and kiss crosses. Some people might say, "Oh, you're weird. You shouldn't kiss a cross. How can you stand the smell of incense?" They're not weird. That's just their spiritual style. Might not be yours, might not be mine, but that doesn't make it wrong if it helps them to connect with God. Some enthusiasts may even enjoy hearing the Bible read in Latin even if they don't understand it. They just feel that this different language connects them with God in some special way.

In the Bible, Ezekiel is an example of a sensate. He talked about the fire and talked about the cloud and connected with God through his senses. Saint John of the Cross would have been someone who was very oriented toward the senses. And in more modern times, my former professor at Harvard, Henri Nouwen, is probably the most famous person in the last fifty years or so who connected with God in this kind of way.

Compassionate

Compassionate people connect with God through service to others, especially to the poor and needy. Instead of finding it tiring or exhausting, they actually find it energizing to serve.

They are constantly looking for new ways to serve and are excited when they find out about a new ministry or a new opportunity where they can help those in need. And this is the way in which they connect with God. They want to feed the hungry. They want to house the homeless. They want to care for the sick. These are their passions.

The compassionate are people that want to be involved in a recovery ministry that helps people get out of addictions, want to be involved in a prison ministry, helping people to come out of prison and get back into society and be able to have a positive life. They are folks that want to be involved in a food pantry. They find that they feel closest to God and feel most connected with God when they are helping and serving others.

In the Bible the Good Samaritan would be a great example of this kind of person. In more historical terms, someone like Mother Theresa or even former President Carter are the kinds of people that are very compassionate in their spiritual style and want to help the poor. Mother Theresa, or Habitat for Humanity, or whatever ministry it may be these are folks that are moving in those directions because they find that's how they connect with God in the best and most significant way.

So the question is: Which style do you identify with? Which style really matches your spiritually? Because there's no right or wrong style. And again, I would say that most people have a predominate and secondary style. For me, my primary style is activist, and my secondary style is intellectual. Those two really are the ways in which I connect with God. So someone like me will rant about people wasting their time watching reality television because the intellectual says you should be reading a book. Someone who is an activist is going to want to preach and proclaim. And you don't have to be a professional to do so.

Also consider the spiritual styles of your husband, wife, sons, daughters, coworkers, and friends. Is your style compatible with theirs? Maybe your differences in style are a source of friction because there's a lack of appreciation and understanding about how you each connect with God. You want to get your praise on, and that's great, but maybe your wife just wants to be alone with God. Recognizing that no style is better than all the others will go a long way toward reconciling clashing spiritual styles.

All of these styles have their strengths and weaknesses. However, having one spiritual style and not another isn't an excuse to adopt an all-or-nothing attitude. For instance, you'd never say, "Well, I don't have the gift of giving so I can't give, or I don't have the gift of serving, so I don't serve." Likewise, you can't say, "Well I'm not an enthusiast, so I come to the services twenty minutes late because I don't want to have to get my praise on." You're not exempt from praising God, enthusiast or not. We're all supposed to praise God.

You might say, "Well, I'm not a compassionate style, so I'm not going to help the poor," but we are *all* supposed

to help the poor. Or you might say, "I'm not a traditionalist, so I'm not into being a church member, tithing, all
that committed stuff." No. We're all supposed to be committed. We're all supposed to tithe. You don't get out of it
by saying I'm not a traditionalist.

So we have to understand and appreciate that we are
still obligated, as Christians, to participate in certain activities that may not complement our spiritual style. For
instance, we all need to read and study the Bible, whether
we're an intellectual or not. We may not have the same
drive or passion for Bible study as an intellectual, but we
all still need to do it. We can't take a pass on things that
don't necessarily resonate with us. We understand there
are certain things that, as a follower of Christ, we all do.

And at the same time, we understand, maybe for the
first time, "Wow. So this is my pathway to connecting
with God. This is my pathway to growing in my relationship with him." If you want to grow in your relationship
with God and experience his presence in a more everyday way, then you need to build on your particular spiritual style. If you're a naturalist, you need to get out into
nature more, not less. If you are an intellectual, you need
to study more. If you are a contemplative, you need to be
alone with God more. If you are an enthusiast, you need
to find ways to praise and worship God more so that you
can draw closer to him and develop your relationship.

What you should feel and what you should experience
when you are moving in your spiritual style is closer to
God. You should feel energized. You should have a kind
of passion that is different, that makes you think to yourself, "Man, this is my sweet spot. This is the place that I
really connect with God, and this is the place I need to

continue to move in, because spiritually I can grow with God through this pathway."

Now, imagine for a moment if everyone did this. Imagine how many people never knew this until right now. You have an opportunity to really take a giant step forward in your growth and connection with God by syncing up with the natural way in which you connect with him best, going down the pathway that leads you to God most easily. How exciting is that? What do you think your spiritual life will look like in the year ahead as you identify your spiritual style and move into it in a greater way? You are likely going to be much more fulfilled spiritually than before. You are going to have a greater excitement and passion about spiritual things and about your relationship with yourself. Others will appreciate connecting with you and growing with you in greater and greater ways.

SPIRITUAL STYLES INVENTORY

- For each statement, mark to what extent it is true of your life:

  3=VERY

  2=SOME

  1=LITTLE

  0=NOT AT ALL

  Put a number in the blank before each statement.

- Transfer the numbers you gave for each statement to the grid at the end of the inventory.

- Total each column. The highest number identifies your preferred spiritual style; the next highest number, your secondary style.

☐ 1. In a church service, I most look forward to the teaching.

☐ 2. People who know me would describe me as enthusiastic during worship times.

☐ 3. I feel closest to God when I'm surrounded by what He has made—the mountains, the forests, or the ocean.

☐ 4. I sense the presence of God most when I'm doing his work.

☐ 5. The most difficult times in my faith are when I can't feel God's presence within me.

☐ 6. I feel closest to God when I see him in the needy, the poor, the sick and the imprisoned.

☐ 7. I feel closest to God when I'm in a church that allows my senses to come alive—when I can see, smell, hear, and almost taste his majesty.

☐ 8. I feel closest to God when I'm participating in a familiar form of worship that evokes memories of my childhood. Rituals and traditions move me more than anything else.

9. I've never understood why people don't love to study the Bible in depth.

10. When I get overwhelmed, there's nothing like a good worship service to get me back on track.

11. When faced with a difficult decision, I am drawn to walk in the woods, on the beach, or in some other outdoor setting.

12. The phrases *courageous confrontation* and *social activism* are very appealing to me.

13. The words *intimacy* and *heart* are very appealing to me.

14. The words *service* and *compassion* are very appealing to me.

15. I enjoy attending a "high church" service with incense and formal Communion or Eucharist.

16. I begin to feel closest to God when I lay something on the altar, giving it for him.

17. The words *concepts* and *truth* are very appealing to me.

18. The words *celebration* and *joy* are very appealing to me.

19. I would rather worship God by spending an hour beside a small brook than by participating in a group.

20. I get frustrated with people's apathy in the face of injustice.

21. I experience a deep inner joy when I am in a quiet place, free from distractions.

22. Helping others is easy for me, even when I have problems.

23. I'd have a difficult time worshiping in a church building that is plain and lacks a sense of awe or majesty. Beauty is very important to me, and I have a difficult time worshiping through second-rate Christian art or music.

24. The words *tradition* and *history* are appealing to me.

25. I spend more money on books than music.

26. I spend more money on music and worship downloads than on books.

27. A beautiful sunset can give me a spiritual high that temporarily blocks out everything bothering me.

☐ 28. People around me know how passionate I feel about the causes I'm involved in.

☐ 29. Spiritual reality sometimes feels more real to me than the physical world.

☐ 30. Even when I'm tired, I find I have the energy and desire to care for people's problems.

☐ 31. The words *colorful* and *aromatic* are appealing to me.

☐ 32. Participating in a formal liturgy or "prayer book" service, developing symbols that I can place in my car, home, or office, and developing a Christian calendar for our family to follow are activities I would enjoy.

☐ 33. Sometimes I spend too much time learning about an issue rather than dealing with it.

☐ 34. God touches me every time I gather with other believers for praise.

☐ 35. Others know that if I'm not around, I'm most likely outside in a beautiful place.

☐ 36. I get tremendous satisfaction from seeing people working together to achieve a goal.

☐ 37. My family and friends sometimes tease me about being such a hermit.

38. I get distracted in meetings or services if I notice details in the surroundings that haven't been attended to.

39. I'm naturally drawn to museums and concerts more than I'm inclined to take a walk in the woods, work in a soup kitchen, or read a book by myself.

40. A book titled *Symbolism and Liturgy in Personal Worship* would be appealing to me.

41. I often real lots of books or articles to help me work through a problem.

42. I like how all the world's problems, including mine, seem unimportant when I'm praising God at church.

43. When I see natural beauty, something wonderful stirs in me that is difficult to describe.

44. I should probably take more time to slow down, but I really love what I do, especially ministry.

45. When I face a difficulty, being alone feels more helpful.

46. I love being able to serve behind the scenes, out of the spotlight.

47. I would really enjoy using drawing exercises, icons, or classical music playing in the background to improve my prayer life.

48. I would really enjoy developing a personal rule (or ritual) of prayer.

1.	2.	3.	4.	5.	6.	7.	8.
9.	10.	11.	12.	13.	14.	15.	16.
17.	18.	19.	20.	21.	22.	23.	24.
25.	26.	27.	28.	29.	30.	31.	32.
33.	34.	35.	36.	37.	38.	39.	40.
41.	42.	43.	44.	45.	46.	47.	48.
Total	Total	Total	Total	Total	Total	Total	Total
Intellectual	Enthusiast	Naturalist	Activists	Contemplative	Compassionate	Sensate	Traditionalist

CHAPTER THREE

PARENTING STYLES

I f you want to start World War III, just go to a family get-together at Thanksgiving or Christmas and question how a couple handles their children. You will see claws come out on even the sweetest sister-in-law. Your own brother, who you have talked with, supported, and harassed your whole life will turn on you like a cobra if you suggest he might be parenting his kids the wrong way.

I have always said there are two things everyone thinks they are great at: lovemaking and driving. Well, parenting is not far behind on this list. Many people think the way they parent their children is the right way—if not the only way. And many do not think they need much help to parent effectively. I base this on my own personal experience with families in my church. We offer classes or groups on a wide range of subjects. Popular topics include having a happy marriage, financial management, physical health, Bible studies, book studies, men's and women's studies, and the list goes on. When we offer a parenting class, though, it is almost always poorly attended. Our parents are speaking with their feet, telling us they either don't want or feel the need for help with their parenting.

The job of parenting is a huge one. I have raised two sons, and I consider it to be one of the hardest jobs of my life. And I have had some tough jobs. I started a church from scratch, which led to starting three more campuses, a preschool, and an afterschool academy. I have written five books on five totally different subjects. I have traveled and spoken on six continents. I did this all while raising those boys. Society is certainly not doing us any favors. Movies, music, and the Internet are all creating challenges previous generations of parents never faced.

There are many different parenting styles, and the style that one parent favors may differ from another parent's style. In his Living With Children column parenting expert Dr. John Rosemond wrote that he believes parenting differences are one of the leading causes of divorce. If two parents have a different style, it can cause a great deal of conflict in a marriage. Rosemond has done informal polls that indicate at least 50 percent of grandparents do not approve of (to varying degrees) how their grandchildren are being raised. The primary complaint he hears from teachers and school administrators is that parents are more likely to disagree than agree with school discipline. Add to all of this parents who don't allow their kids to play at other children's homes because of parenting differences. Different parenting styles are fracturing marriages, families, and friendships. Identifying and understanding your parenting style is the first step in preventing clashes and promoting healing, supportive relationships.

Helicopter

The term "helicopter" speaks of both the hovering nature of some parents and their propensity to swoop in to the rescue. This parent hovers over their child at the playground, micromanages their kid's play dates, and essentially oversees all aspects of their child's life. They are not just involved, they are over-involved. The parent tries to shelter or control the child's environment. They tell their children how they should think and feel. Cell phones have increased this parenting style and have essentially become the world's longest umbilical cords. Now parents can talk to and keep tabs on their kids almost at will.

This type of parent sometimes continues to hover beyond high school and interferes with their young adults' lives. In an interview with TechCrunch (June 30, 2015) former Stanford University Dean Julie Lythcott-Haims claims parents are quite involved in college students' lives. She has witnessed parents registering their kid for classes, settling roommate disputes, and talking to their kid's professors. She believes that when too much is done for children, it actually makes them less capable. The desire to do things for themselves can be lost, as can the motivation to do the hard work that's necessary for success.

Parental involvement can even go beyond college and infiltrate the workplace. According a *Harvard Business Review* blog post (Willyerd 2013) "Parents May Be Your Secret Weapon for Recruiting and Retaining Millennials," parents are increasingly involved in their millennial child's career. In fact, they advocate for companies to utilize parents as allies in recruiting or retaining their children. Their advice includes inviting parents to new employee orientation in order to strengthen the employee bond by helping parents understand their brand. Another strategy is holding a "Take Your Parents to Work" day like the one recently held by LinkedIn. They even encourage subscribing parents to the company newsletter or other communications to keep them engaged in their kid's company culture. Parents can thus rescue their kid's before they hurt their career.

With this style, a parent swoops in to rescue their child from whatever problem they may be encountering. They step in at the first sign of discomfort or challenge. In a school situation, the parent will communicate to the teacher in various ways that her child needs to get a certain grade, usually an A. Many teachers have personally told me about this dynamic happening over and over again. In fact, they feel the pressure today is greater from the parents than from students.

When a child procrastinates until the last minute to do a project the helicopter parent intervenes. Instead of letting the child suffer the consequences of their procrastination, the parent steps in to save the day. Helicopter parents will do almost anything for their child, including racing to Hobby Lobby, Walmart or the nearest craft store to do the project. These parents are so adept at school crafts that the child inevitably gets an A, and the parent is a hero. The child has learned nothing except that Mom or Dad will rescue them from their problems.

Helicopter parents are also prone to the faulty belief that it is never their child's fault when something happens or goes wrong. These parents will verbally defend their child's actions, right or wrong. They will redefine the child's behavior. The child is not selfish—they always share. If there is a problem, it is always somebody else. In their eyes, their child is perfect and can do no wrong. We all love our kids, but natural logic should lead us to know that they can and will screw up. If we consider how we are sometimes prone to making mistakes, it's likely that our child is as well.

More importantly, if we rescue them from all their problems, they will never learn how to deal with issues and difficulties on their own. They'll never learn how to resolve conflict themselves or that their actions have consequences. That is harmful and will have long-term negative consequences. Helicopter parents aren't doing their kids any favors because some day they are going to work for a boss who does not care what their mom or dad thinks. Parents cannot always rescue their children. There can be a fine line between helpful parenting and helicopter parenting, between mothering and smothering. If a child needs help, the goal should be to help them deal with it rather than figuring out a way to take care of it for them.

Attachment

The attachment style is based on the parent's singular desire to establish a strong emotional bond with their child. The family is really centered on the children. Parents with this style believe they should promptly respond to their child's needs, whatever they may be. They want to be sensitive and emotionally available to their child at all times. The goal of this type of parenting is for the child to become a secure, peace-loving, and empathetic adult. The effectiveness of this parenting style has been studied and researched by some pediatricians. There are even attachment-parenting laboratories and mother-baby sleep laboratories focused on encouraging this parenting style.

This style places special importance on the role of the mother. Natural childbirth is the way attachment moms bring their children into the world. Mothers are inspired to "wear" their babies for up to a year. Baby-wearing is done by carrying an infant in a sling, which functions as "transitional womb" for the new baby. Moms are also encouraged to breastfeed, usually till the child is three years old. These parents practice co-sleeping, where the mom, dad and all the children sleep together or are welcome in the parents' bed. These practices are a part of some indigenous cultures, and attachment parents want to return to a simpler, more natural way of family life.

Among adherents of the attachment style, home-schooling is popular. From their perspective, the more time these parents can spend bonding with their children, the better. These parents avoid any type of corporal punishment since they feel it would defeat their goal of security and peace. Some of these parents are also part of the anti-vaccination movement.

The role of the father and his relationship with his wife is an issue in this parenting style. So much work and energy fall to the mother that the role of the father is diminished. Moms sometimes begin to act like their husbands are no longer as important and almost part of a previous way of living. The mother surrenders her life to her children and their needs. The needs of the husband can be ignored or minimized. This can lead to problems in the marriage and even result in divorce. A more natural style of parenting should lead to strengthening the family and certainly the marriage at its foundation.

Permissive

The permissive style involves parents indulging their children. The goal is to provide an environment without restraints. They make very few demands, set very few rules, and have very few expectations for their children. These parents rarely discipline their children in any way because they have no rules that must be obeyed. They have low expectations of their children for practicing self-control or mature behavior. Responding to the children rather than demanding a response from them is what this parenting style is all about.

These parents want to be buddies with their kids. They want to be friends with their child. This style can be easily adopted in single-parent families. A single parent will sometimes compensate for their lack of a spouse by communicating with their child like an adult. The parent can take on the role of friend more than that of parent. This makes discipline and confrontations about behavior very challenging for the parent, and they may rarely address these issues. They will use bribery to motivate their child's outward behavior. Permissive parents are often more concerned with getting a desired outward behavior rather than an inner attitude transformation. The parent and the child both see the parent as being lenient.

Rosemond said, "A parent cannot provide proper leadership if the parent's energies are focused primarily on having a wonderful relationship with a child." Permissive parents don't have to be an enemy of their child, but they don't have to be the child's best friend either. Friendship may come later, after they are grown adults. It can be an incredible blessing to have that closeness, but it's not practical until children have reached adulthood.

Permissive parenting by one parent but not the other can create conflict. The permissive parent allows eating in the family room while the other parent allows only eating at the table. The permissive parent stretches the bedtime schedule by an hour or more while the other parent adheres to it. The permissive parent buys chips and candy while the other parent limits high-sugar/fat items. The children see the permissive parent as their buddy or friend but then the other parent can become the mean one or the bad guy.

Permissive parents hold democratic family meetings. The parents want their children to see this egalitarian approach as a democratic opportunity for debate and consensus. These meetings are not to share information or resolve conflict. Rather, everyone is gathered together and everyone has an equal vote. While there is nothing wrong with discussion, it can be difficult to reason with a child who does not have the same knowledge, experience, and maturity as an adult. It is simply unfair to set them up for defeat. There can and should be a lot of discussion and input during the family decision-making process. However, the parent should have the final say after they've listened to everyone's input. Once the decision is made, that is the decision to which the family adheres.

The permissive style often leads to children who have problems with authority and self-regulation.

Domineering

On the other end of the parenting spectrum is the domineering style. In this style, children are expected to follow the strict rules of their parents. Failure to follow the rules usually results in punishment. There is a high expectation of morality and intolerance to rationalizations or excuses. These parents do not explain the rationale for many of their rules or decisions. They see the children as subservient and see themselves as having total authority.

The parent controls many aspects of the children's lives. Their excessive demands discourage the child's personal initiative. They have high demands but are not necessarily responsive to their children's needs. The expression of love is not highly valued. Anger is an emotion most likely to be expressed by the parents. A domineering parent is quick to punish but is not emotionally responsive. They may talk to their kids in a harsh or punitive manner. These parents simply expect their orders to be obeyed without explanation.

Children raised this way tend to be more obedient and even proficient. However, they can respond with rebellion in various ways. They may overeat, perform poorly in school, or get involved with drugs. These kids may make choices based on what other people think and not what they think themselves. They're potentially more susceptible to peer pressure.

There is also the issue of confidence and self-esteem. Children who are raised by domineering parents can lack confidence in their decision-making. Because they have been ordered around their whole lives, they have not developed the skills for making decisions or the confidence to take risks.

Disconnected

Some may say disconnected parenting is not a style since it indicates a lack of connection with children, but it is a style for some parents. It's characterized by a lack of involvement in parenting. The parents place few demands on the children, they are somewhat unresponsive, and there is little communication. Though the parents meet the child's basic needs, they are generally detached from the life of their child.

These parents simply do not provide any structure for their children. The lack of communication keeps the children from knowing rules and limits. The lack of parental action shows them there is no real concern for their welfare. For some parents, this style is a result of marital circumstances. When there is a divorce and there are difficulties spending time with the children, this can become the default mode of parenting. Certain careers like military service or traveling sales make it almost impossible to have regular input into a child's life. If a parent is not around enough, they may not really know what their children are doing.

Some parents were raised with this style, so they parent the way they were parented. That's also why children raised in an orphanage or in a foster home may choose this style. Based by their own upbringing, they may define parental responsibility differently than others. This style can lead to neglect or even rejection of the children's needs. As a result, kids can develop low self-esteem, lack self-control, and be less competent than their peers.

Authoritative

Authoritative parents establish rules and guidelines and expect their children to follow them. These parents are responsive to their children and are willing to listen to them. But they do believe in the motto, "You live under my roof, you follow my rules." This parenting style exhibits both love and structure. The children are raised to believe they are special and have God-given potential and an important purpose. The structure of their family life provides the boundaries that they need. The boundaries relieve the pressure of making choices and facing situations for which they are not prepared.

When children fail to meet expectations, there are consequences, but the discipline is more redemptive than punitive. The parents communicate clear standards for their child's conduct. They are assertive but not overly demanding. These parents can deal with a child's anger over not letting them have their way. They love their children but they will say no to them when needed.

The authoritative style is based on parental authority. In an interview (Hawkins Adams 2016), family physician Dr. Leonard Sax said, "Teaching right and wrong is one of the central jobs of parents and you have to teach from a position of authority." These parents exercise authority and manage the family lifestyle. This includes routines such as having a regular dinner time with every member of the family free of all electronic devices. Limiting the amount of time spent watching television. Intentionally keeping the calendar from being overscheduled so there is family time. In many ways this parenting style is about strong leadership, shaping culture, and building character. A leader is decisive, purposeful, determined, commanding, and visionary. This describes the parent with an authoritative style.

A parental leader does not plead, bargain, bribe, or explain. Thus, children do not complain, argue, or disobey very often. The parent delivers instructions fully upright rather than crouching down to the child's level. This parent uses as few words as possible—the more concise the instruction, the more authoritative it sounds. They do not explain because that stimulates arguments. They do not end the instructions with "okay?" as if agreement is needed. And when the instructions have been delivered, the parent simply walks away, confident there is no need to see if what has been instructed will be done.

There is another element of authoritative parenting that is unique. Although it may seem counterintuitive, these parents make their marriage the top priority in parenting. They have a couple-centered rather than a child-centered family. A couple-centered family will result in a stronger marriage, which will result in a healthier family. The worst outcome for a family is to experience divorce, and the best way to prevent divorce to is to prioritize and focus on the marriage.

Massachusetts Mutual Life did a survey in their *Family Fun Magazine* about parenting. Many parents reported spending as much time with their children as the children want and need. However, they felt they needed more time with their spouses. About half the parents surveyed felt they did not have enough time with their spouses, indicating they are giving parenting more priority than time with their spouse. The marriage is what's more important. These parents are "in love" with their spouse and they love their children. They are not "in love" with their children. It is not that they don't love their kids. It is merely a proper understanding of the nature of the relationship. Authoritative parents want the children to know that they love them, but they are in love with their spouse. Authoritative parents have a clear goal in their parenting: raising self-sufficient, independent adults. The entire time they are parenting, they are working themselves out of a job.

The US Census Bureau American Housing Survey found that almost 16 million families have at least one child over the age of eighteen living at home. Fifty-seven percent of college graduates now are living in their parent's house. The reasoning is that they are retreating from the high housing costs, burdensome college debt, and a tough job market.

Authoritative parents would perceive their child moving back home after college as a failure of parental leadership. Their goal is to raise children to be independent and self-sufficient so they can go out and meet the challenges of life—not so they can retreat and come back home. The Survey also stated twenty-five percent of adults ages 40 through 70 expect their young adult children to move back in with them at some point. This 25 percent is not practicing the authoritative style of parenting. In general, authoritative parents produce children who are happy, capable, and successful.

. . . . .

No matter the parenting style, the mission of every parent is to raise a resilient child, who becomes a mature adult dealing with the challenges, hardships, and problems of life. The classic definition of maturity is the ability to delay gratification and the ability to tolerate frustration. The combination creates a mentally healthy, mature adult. A parent raises their child to understand some gratification has to be delayed. They help their child to understand they will have to tolerate the frustrations of life.

Parenting styles will vary. The causes of these differences include culture, personality, parental background, family size, socio-economic status, educational level, and religion. Differing parenting styles within a family creates a unique blend and challenge. If a mother displays a permissive style and a father favors an authoritative style, there will be a need for compromise and cooperation. A cohesive approach to parenting is crucial for family effectiveness.

The role of parents is paramount, and the responsibility lies squarely on their shoulders for the health of the family. Evaluate your parenting style and your spouse's style. Although you might be tempted to share this chapter with your neighbor, friend, or sibling, first consider your own family. You, your spouse, and your children will be the beneficiaries.

PARENTING STYLES INVENTORY

- For each statement, mark to what extent it is true of your life:

  3=VERY

  2=SOME

  1=LITTLE

  0=NOT AT ALL

  Put the number in the blank before each statement.

- Transfer the numbers you gave for each statement to the grid at the end of the inventory.

- Total each column. The highest number identifies your preferred parenting style; the next highest number, your secondary style.

1. I oversee all aspects of my child's life by telling them how they should think and feel.

2. My family centers around the children.

3. I try not to set rules for my kids.

4. I have very strict rules that my children need to follow.

☐ 5. I don't think parenting requires much involvement or communication with my children.

☐ 6. I have rules and guidelines that my children must follow.

☐ 7. I want to be involved in my millennial's career.

☐ 8. As a mother, natural childbirth was the way to go as this is more "natural" way.

☐ 9. I believe parents and their kids should be buddies—friends.

☐ 10. I am the parent and my children need to follow my rules.

☐ 11. My children's lives are very unstructured.

☐ 12. My children believe they are special and have God-given potential and an important purpose.

☐ 13. I don't mind helping my child complete a project if he has procrastinated until the last minute.

☐ 14. I prefer homeschooling to public or private school.

☐ 15. I like to have family meetings with my kids.

☐ 16. I think my children need to follow my rules, no questions asked.

☐ 17. I don't like to put demands on my children.

☐ 18. I communicate clear standards for my children's conduct.

☐ 19. I think my child is close to perfect, and it is usually another's fault when something goes wrong.

☐ 20. As a father, I feel my role in raising our children is not important.

☐ 21. Sometimes I don't agree with my spouse on expected behavior for our child.

☐ 22. My children are very susceptible to peer pressure.

☐ 23. My children show characteristics of low self-esteem, lack of self-control, and are less competent than their peers.

☐ 24. I have a couple-centered approach to parenting.

1.	2.	3.	4.	5.	6.
7.	8.	9.	10.	11.	12.
13.	14.	15.	16.	17.	18.
19.	20.	21.	22.	23.	24.
Total	Total	Total	Total	Total	Total
Helicopter	Attachment	Permissive	Domineering	Disconnected	Authoritative

CHAPTER FOUR

DECISION STYLES

There have been a lot of bad decisions through-out history. In 1979, Bill Gates went to Ross Perot and offered to sell him Microsoft, his young fledgling company. Some say the price was as low as $6 million, and others say it was as high as $60 million. Either way, Ross Perot would have made millions of dollars if he had bought the company. But he didn't.

Years before that bad decision, Sam Phillips, who owned a small recording studio in Memphis, Tennessee, signed a young man named Elvis Presley. And then RCA Records offered to buy his studio and everyone he had under contract for $35,000. It seemed like a lot of money, so Sam sold his studio and contracts, including Elvis's contract, and ultimately forfeited millions of dollars in royalties as Elvis went on to sell billions of records.

The Munich Technical Institute turned down a young aspiring student because they said he showed no real promise as a scientist. His name was Albert Einstein. It turns out he was a pretty good scientist.

Other bad decisions include New Coke and leisure suits. Leisure suits were a very bad decision. I think the AMC Pacer was a bad decision and the Gremlin too. I think that entire car company sort of fell into bad decision-making somewhere along the line.

Genesis 2:15–16 says,

> The LORD God put the man in the Garden of Eden to take care of it and look after it. But the LORD told him, "You may eat fruit from any tree in the garden except the one that has the power to let you know the difference between right and wrong. If you eat any fruit from that tree, you will die before the day is over!"

Then in 3:6,

> The woman stared at the fruit. It looked beautiful and tasty. She wanted the wisdom that it would give her. And so she ate some of the fruit. Her husband was there with her, so she gave some to him, and he ate it too.

Every other bad decision pales in comparison to this one. When Adam and Eve made the decision to disobey God, it changed the course of human history. However, because of Jesus, we've been redeemed from the curse of sin. We're set free. We can be forgiven. That is the great gospel message. It is the message of Christianity.

Our decision style influences the way we make decisions. Understanding your unique style will make you aware of the pitfalls that might lead you to bad decision-making. Your decision style could be holding you back from God's best for your life. It could be keeping you from making the right decision—or making any decision at all. No matter your style, It's important to avoid mistakes and make the best possible decisions.

Overthinker

An overthinker is someone who collects lots of information but doesn't ever make a decision. Their hope is that if they get enough information, making the decision will be extremely easy. But after considering every possible angle, they still hesitate to make a decision.

That kind of hesitation can lead to missing opportunities that could otherwise bless your life. Lee Iacocca said it best years ago: "Even the right decision is the wrong decision if it's made too late." If someone hesitates and never makes a decision, then even what could have been the right decision ends up turning out to be the wrong decision.

In the Bible, Moses is an example of an overthinker. The story of his indecision about leading the Israelites is found in Exodus 4:

> Moses asked the LORD, "Suppose everyone refuses to listen to my message and no one believes that you really appeared to me?" The LORD answered, "What's that in your hand?" "A walking stick," Moses replied. "Throw it down!" the LORD commanded. So Moses threw the stick on the ground. It immediately turned into a snake, and Moses jumped back. "Pick it

up by the tail!" the LORD told him. And when
Moses did this. the snake turned back into a
walking stick. "Do this," the LORD said, "and
the Israelites will believe that you've seen me"
(vv. 1–5).

You would think that having a stick that turned into a
snake would be enough to seal the deal for Moses, but it
was not. In fact, Moses replied, "I have never been a good
speaker. I wasn't one before you spoke to me, and I'm not
one now" (v. 10). Moses did not think he was leadership
material, but God answered,

"Who makes people able to speak or makes
them deaf or unable to speak? Who gives them
sight or makes them blind? Don't you know
I'm the one who does these things? Now go!
When you speak, I'll be with you and I'll give
you the words to say" (vv. 11–12).

After such strong encouragement, one would assume
the decision had been made. But Moses's response was
"LORD, please send someone else to do it" (v. 13). He
kept getting information—good information—that he
was God's chosen leader, but Moses kept hesitating. He
could not make the decision to lead.

If you are one of these people who overthinks
everything, keeps collecting information and collecting
information but doesn't come to a place of making a
decision, you are lacking trust. You need to trust yourself
and trust that God is guiding you and directing you to
make the right call.

Moses wasn't able to do that. Ultimately, he ended up getting his brother, Aaron, to be his spokesman—to do what he should have been doing himself. Don't miss out on the good things God has for you because you are unable or unwilling to be decisive. Trust God, trust the research, trust yourself, and make the decision.

Impulsive

A person with an impulsive decision-making style really doesn't want to do anything that the overthinker does. They are not interested in collecting or processing information. Impulsive decision-makers simply want to decide and to decide quickly.

Checkout counters are set up to encourage impulsive individuals to engage in impulse buying. Product marketers strive to grab people's attention while they're standing in line so they'll say, "Oh, wow. You just water this plant and it grows into some sort of shape? This sounds great. I should definitely buy it." Or "Oh, Angelina Jolie is doing this new movie and getting another tattoo? I need to know this information. Five dollars? No problem. It's worth it!" Or "I used to like Butterfingers when I was a kid. I haven't had one of those in a while. Ooh, it's in a special supersize. I think I'll take that."

Later they might regret their impulsive decision and think, "What am I doing with this giant Butterfinger?" Or "Who cares how many tattoos Angelina Jolie has?"

Peter, one of Jesus's twelve disciples, made many impulsive decisions in the Bible. When Jesus appeared to the disciples at night in the middle of the sea, Peter jumped out of the boat and started walking on water while everyone else decided to stay in the boat. Peter was also the one who, when a Roman cohort of over 600 men came to arrest Jesus, grabbed a sword and cut off one soldier's ear. And when he was with James, John, and Jesus on the Mount of Transfiguration and had this incredible spiritual experience, he suggested building a worship center immediately. He didn't take time to consider how else they might remember or memorialize the occasion. When Jesus told the disciples he was going down a path of pain and suffering, it was Peter who impulsively told Jesus that was not going to happen. If you are one of these impulsive decision-makers, you're in the company of a great leader in the early church.

Impulsive individuals should wait before acting and avoid making quick decisions. Wait to get more information. Wait till your emotions come down three or four notches. Put the brakes on. Respect the stop sign. Let your intellect come into play and make the right decision.

Fun Seeker

Fun seekers base their decisions on whatever is most enjoyable or will be the most pleasurable. They don't think about all of the factors. If it's going to be fun and enjoyable, then the decision is yes. If there are ramifications, they rationalize that those can be dealt with later.

The fun factor cannot be all you consider when making a decision. I have garnered a reputation for leading a church that believes you can have fun and serve God. I think you can do both as long as it's understood that fun is a secondary goal when it comes to serving God. Having your priorities in order is key to good decision-making.

Samson is a great biblical example of a fun seeker. He was legendary for his feats of strength and his wild actions. In Judges 14, Samson saw a woman and wanted her. He tells his dad to go get her for him so they can marry. However, she was a Philistine, and her people were the mortal enemies of the Israelites. God is very clear that believers shouldn't intermarry with nonbelievers, so Samson should have never pursued marrying a Philistine. Nonetheless, Samson decides to have a bachelor party and tells thirty of the Philistine men it will last seven days.

Samson also tells the men a riddle, and if they can tell him the right answer before the party is over, he agrees to give each man a shirt and a full change of clothing. But if they can't tell him the answer, then each of them will have to give him a shirt and a full change of clothing. Wanting to win the bet, the Philistines went to Sampson's future bride and said, "You had better trick your husband into telling you the answer to his riddle. Have you invited us here just to rob us? If you don't find out the answer, we'll burn you and your family to death" (Judges 14:15). Samson's bride went to him, crying, and told him that if he loved her, he would tell her the answer to his riddle. For the entire seven days she kept whining and trying to get the answer from him. On the seventh day, she put so much pressure on Samson that he finally gave in and told her the answer. Judges 14:17 says, "She went straight to the young men and told them."

The thirty guys then tell Sampson that they know the answer to the riddle, and Sampson gets so mad that he goes out and kills thirty other guys, takes their clothes, and brings their clothes to these thirty guys. He went back to get his fiancé, but her father actually gave her to be married to one of the thirty guys because he thought Sampson was so mad that he wouldn't want to be married to her anymore. Sampson was so mad that he decided to burn a bunch of Philistine vineyards and orchards. The Philistines wanted to kill Samson for all the trouble he had caused, and the Israelites went to Sampson and told him they were going to turn him in. Three thousand Philistines showed up to take Sampson, and as soon as they let him go, he broke free of the ropes restraining him, grabbed the jawbone of a dead animal and killed all 3,000 men.

Where did this whole ugly saga start? It started with his fun-seeking decision to marry the wrong woman. Fun seekers need to obey and understand that the principles of the Bible are for our good. God's not a killjoy. He's not trying to keep you from fun. He's trying to protect you from getting into situations that will complicate your life or cause you harm, difficulty, and despair. The fun seeker needs to make decisions based on the principles and teachings of the Bible.

Non-Confronter

The non-confronter is someone who can't decide to do something because they might possibly upset someone. This is your people-pleasing person. They really just want people to like them and want everybody to be happy and get along. But everybody can't be happy and everybody can't get along. Sometimes decisions have to be made that favor one group or person over another.

Timothy was a protégé of the apostle Paul and a non-confronter. Paul was trying to develop him into a great

leader of the church, and he wrote several letters to him
about what's needed in a leader. These letters comprise 1
Timothy and 2 Timothy in the Bible. In 2 Timothy 1:7–8
Paul wrote,

> God's spirit doesn't make cowards out of us.
> The Spirit gives us power, love, and self-con-
> trol. Don't be ashamed to speak for our LORD.

And in 2 Timothy 2:1–2, he wrote,

> Timothy, my child, Christ Jesus is kind, and
> you must let him make you strong. You have
> often heard me teach. Now I want you to tell
> these same things to followers who can be
> trusted to tell others.

Paul was telling Timothy that he had to say the hard
things. He needed to decide to tell people what they
needed to hear. Likewise, God hasn't given you a spirit
of timidity either. Everyone may not like, agree with, or
appreciate what you have to say, but you must be willing
to say the things that need to be said anyway. You may
have to make decisions that aren't popular. But you have
to do it. Any good leader knows this.

So the non-confronter needs to have courage—the
courage to decide and make the tough call when it needs
to be made. The non-confronting style is a very poor way
to make decisions, because you can't make everyone happy. One of my mentors said to me, "If you try to make
everyone happy, you'll end up making hardly anyone

happy." Sometimes it takes some courage to make tough decisions.

Procrastinator

The procrastinator puts off decisions for as long as they can. They secretly hope that if they keep putting off the decision, they will never actually have to make one. They think circumstances and events will transpire and decisions will be made, but they won't have to make them.

Someone in the Bible who exhibited this style was a Roman governor named Felix. He was someone who the apostle Paul interacted with when he was placed in prison for his ministry. The story is in Acts 24:24–25:

> Several days later, Felix and his wife Drusilla, who was Jewish, went to the place where Paul was kept under guard. They sent for Paul and listened while he spoke to them about having faith in Christ Jesus. But Felix was frightened when Paul started talking to them about doing right, about self-control, and about the coming judgment. So he said to Paul, "That's enough for now. You may go. When I have time I will send for you."

Felix did not want to make a decision at that moment. He wanted to put it off for another time—a decision about faith and Christ. He said he would talk to Paul later, but that never happened. The Bible tells us nothing about Felix ever calling Paul back again. The old adage is absolutely true: Not making a decision is a decision.

In deciding not act, procrastinators leave the decision-making to someone else.

What is fascinating about Felix's story is that it revolves around the most important decision a person can make: having faith in God and beginning to follow Jesus's lead. When you choose Jesus, your life takes an enormous turn for the better. You immediately gain inner peace, begin to discover God's plan for your life, and have a true purpose for living. If you were to die unexpectedly, you would spend eternity in heaven with Jesus. Remember that no one is guaranteed a long life—sickness and disease can visit any person. Second Corinthians 6:2 (NLT) tells us "today is the day of salvation." Don't procrastinate on the most important decision of your life.

The procrastinator needs to act and decide now—especially in regard to following Christ. That is the most important decision, but there are many other big decisions a person must make. Perhaps you have been dating the same person for years. It is time to decide if this is the person you want to marry. You may have delayed moving to a new home or area because you can't make up your mind. You know what you want to do, and it's time to make the decision. It's time to act. And after you do, you are going to be so happy you finally took the step that you needed to take.

Wisdom Seeker

Wisdom seekers look to others for wisdom before making a decision. There are many sources of information on social media and across the Internet, but not all information is wisdom. *Parade* magazine had a cover story featuring advice about mothering. But the advice did not come from mothers who have done an outstanding and excellent job. Instead it came from television mothers— the actresses who play mothers on TV are giving out wisdom about parenting!

King Solomon is a biblical example of a wisdom seeker. In I Kings 3:5 we read, "The LORD God . . . said, 'Solomon, ask for anything you want and I will give it to you.' " Imagine God giving you the opportunity to ask for anything in the whole world. What would you ask for? In verse 9 we read what Solomon asked for: "Please make me wise." Solomon chose wisdom above wealth, fame, or long life. By choosing wisdom, he gained all of those and more through his wise decisions. As king of the greatest empire in his day, he needed wisdom—especially since he was young and had just replaced his famous father, David.

The wisdom seeker forms a team of people who can serve as advisors. We start out life with a preordained team of advisors called parents, teachers, and coaches. They are there to give us advice to make wise decisions. These are different kinds of people who have had different experiences, both negative and positive. As we get older, the need for wisdom and counsel does not go away. You may need a financial advisor to help with decisions about finances, planning for retirement, and making good investments. You may need a physical trainer to help you take care of your body and live healthy. You need trusted friends who know you and can advise you with your best interests in mind. The advice they give could spare you from heartache or the negative consequences of a bad decision, or it could lead you to a really good situation. You could make a marvelous decision because of a piece of wise advice or an insightful perspective that was shared with you.

The wisdom seeker looks for situational counsel when making a decision. Different situations require the input of different people. You may be tempted to seek out advice until someone tells you what you want to hear. You can do that, but it's not going to work well. You have to be able to listen, process the advice, and determine the best course of action. Seek out credentialed individuals or experts when necessary. If you are ready to make a decision but don't know what the Bible has to say about your particular situation, speak with someone who has lots of biblical knowledge, who can tell you what the Bible teaches, or at least some of the principles that the Bible provides for this situation. Find someone who has already made the decision and seen the results. Before getting married, for instance, seek out successful married couples. Before making a large purchase, talk to someone who knows the product. Before accepting a job offer, talk to someone who has worked there for years. The wisdom seeker always seeks wisdom before making decisions and benefits greatly from it.

. . . . .

While most people often favor one particular decision style, they could be influenced by more than one style depending on the situation and the particular decision that needs to be made. It is crucial to understand your decision style, especially when it comes to your most important decision: having faith in Jesus Christ. If you still haven't made that decision to step forward and exercise your faith, now is the time to decide. Make the decision to believe in Jesus, to make him the leader of your life, and to receive his forgiveness for your sins. I want to help you in making that decision with a prayer:

Jesus, today I'm making a decision to follow you, to make you the leader of my life. I acknowledge I am far from perfect and that I need your forgiveness for all my past sins, mistakes, and failures. I receive your forgiveness today, and I ask you to make me a new and better person from this day forward. I choose to follow your leading and direction, believing that your purpose and plan for my life is what will lead me to the greatest happiness and peace. In your name, amen.

DECISION STYLES INVENTORY

- For each statement, mark to what extent it is true of your life:

  3=VERY

  2=SOME

  1=LITTLE

  0=NOT AT ALL

- Put a number in the blank before each statement.

- Transfer the numbers you gave for each statement to the grid at the end of the inventory.

- Total each column. The highest number identifies your preferred decision style; the next highest number, your secondary style.

☐ 1. I find it challenging to make a decision.

☐ 2. I find it easy to make a decision.

☐ 3. The only information I need to make a decision is if it will be pleasurable and fun for me.

☐ 4. I am a people pleaser and don't want my decisions to upset anyone.

☐ 5. I put off making a decision as long as I can so hopefully I won't have to make it.

☐ 6. I like to seek wisdom from others before making a decision.

☐ 7. In order to make a decision, I gather as much information as I can.

☐ 8. I like to make quick decisions without much information.

☐ 9. Sometimes my wishes for pleasure and fun get me into difficult situations.

☐ 10. I am usually not willing to make a difficult decision.

☐ 11. I find that by not making a decision now, someone else will make it for me.

☐ 12. I have a team of advisors who helps me make wise decisions.

☐ 13. In making a decision, I tend to overthink the issue.

☐ 14. Sometimes my emotions cause me to act or react quickly.

☐ 15. I find decision-making does not involve much research.

☐ 16. I find it difficult to say things that other people really need to hear even though they need to be said.

☐ 17. Sometimes by putting off a decision, I find a decision is never made.

☐ 18. When I need to make a decision, I seek situational counsel from others who have the expertise to help with that specific decision.

1.	2.	3.	4.	5.	6.
7.	8.	9.	10.	11.	12.
13.	14.	15.	16.	17.	18.
Total	Total	Total	Total	Total	Total
Overthinker	Impulsive	Fun Seeker	Non-Confronter	Procrastinator	Wisdom Seeker

CHAPTER FIVE

WORK STYLES

The US Bureau of Labor Statistics has determined that by the time an average American is forty years old he will have held 10.5 jobs. I'm not sure what holding half a job is, but I think it might have something to do with averages. If you think about your life from age eighteen to age forty (if you are that old), it's amazing how many different jobs you can have.

How do you see work? Some people see work as a necessary evil. They don't really want to do it. They don't really even like it. They may not have a very positive attitude or perspective on the nature and value of work. But they understand work is necessary in order to have money.

Other people see work as a cruel master. They do their job because it is required of them. They have a boss—they have responsibilities. They would rather be doing other things. They could be having fun, but instead they have to work. This kind of mentality sees work as hard. Work is a master that drives them, but there is nothing they can do about it.

For others, their job defines them. They are good at their work, and it makes them feel important. Everything in their life revolves around their job. They don't have any work/life balance. Their life is really all about the job, and just the job.

Genesis 2:15 (NIV) says: "The LORD God took the man and put him in the Garden of Eden to work it and to take care of it." (It is important to note this is chapter 2– things don't get all messed up until the next chapter, when sin enters the world.) God had a plan from the beginning that we would be workers. Why do we work? Work reveals our partnership with God. He is a worker and has given us an opportunity to be a worker as well. And together we can do something God wants to get done. God has given us the responsibility to work on caring for this earth, humanity, and everything that is in our lives. We are in partnership with God. We help God carry out his plan and purpose for this world.

He has multiple plans and multiple purposes that he is trying to accomplish around the world, and God uses each of us. The grocer supplies the food. The lawyer brings justice. The homemaker nurtures the children. The teacher educates. God is using all people in different ways to do his work. And it is good to be in partnership with God in whatever role you find yourself.

It is good to be able to work in a factory and make items people need in order to do other work that needs to get done. It is good to work in the IT field since our world is so unbelievably dependent upon technology and computing. It is good to work in an office and make sure business is getting done; orders are taken, sales are closed, and goods are delivered. All this work is important and necessary. And all work done with ethics and integrity ultimately glorifies God.

Jesus said in John 5:17 (NIV), "My Father is always at his work to this very day, and I too am working." God is working. Jesus was working when he was on this earth. Work is what we do. Workers are who we are. Work is not a curse. It is not bad. Work is not some kind of cruel master that we have to serve. Work is what God created us to do. It is not all we are to do. It is not all of who we are, but it does reveal our partnership with God.

Whatever your job, you are working in partnership with God to achieve whatever it is God wants done. Sometimes it is hard to fully grasp the complexity of how things work together in order for something to get accomplished. But God knows. He understands. We have a role. We have a place. You never know how what you are doing may end up impacting other people's lives in a positive way.

Finding the right role or place is crucial for your work to be fulfilling. Being the right person for the right assignment makes all the difference in your performance. In order to determine this, you must identify your work style. Your work should be what you want to do, not what you have done before, not what you feel needs to be done, and not what you think others expect you to do.

When your work style is matched with your work role, you'll find incredible self-fulfillment. Discovering your work style leads to true self-acceptance. You'll feel good about who you are and working the way you feel most comfortable. Discerning your work style releases your natural energy, allowing you to maximize your work production. You are doing what you want to do rather than what you have to do. Doing something else besides your job is not as appealing because your job energizes you.

Once you determine your work style, declining offers for positions or jobs for which you would not be suited becomes so much easier. You can recognize immediately and accurately the roles where you will find the greatest fulfillment and the least frustration. Functioning on the team where your style is the right fit leads to increased unity and performance.

The amount of time, money, and energy saved by identifying your work style is enormous—to both you and your employer. To quote a Jim Collins mantra, "Getting the right person, in the right seat, on the right bus" is the goal of every successful organization. Understanding your work style and that of others on your team helps to decide easily and quickly who fits where in a given role or position. It also aids tremendously in making the best hiring decisions. As you and others are in the right role for your work style, burnout and turnover will be significantly reduced.

Understanding how you and your coworkers differ in your work styles creates a healthy environment of mutual acceptance and support. Frustrations are lessened and respect is enhanced. Appreciation for the strengths of each person's style results in a more harmonious workplace and a deeper level of understanding.

Work styles are different from work strengths. Millions are aware of or have even taken the Strengths Finder Assessment (Rath 2007). Gallup researchers have spent more than a decade doing interviews, studies and surveys trying to understand human talents. They have uncovered thirty-four key patterns of feeling, thought, and behavior, categorizing them with names like Relator, Visionary, or Achiever. These themes identify a person's innate and unique talents. When these talents are practiced and developed, they become a person's strengths.

That's why Identifying your strengths is very valuable and can even help you in your work style, but they are not the same. Almost forty years ago, Bobb Biehl developed a Role Preference Inventory (now called Team Profile) to help people and organizations find the best role for a person on a team (Biehl 2005). He classified work into a five-phase developmental process. He believed a person has only one phase in which he most enjoys working, referring to that phase as a role preference. I call it a work style.

Designer

The ideal job assignment for the designer style is one where she can design a totally new, unique approach to a theoretical problem that provides a creative solution. Starting from scratch with original concepts and models, the designer thinks more theoretically than practically. She wants to find fresh ways to unlock an idea, whether it's hers or someone else's. She wants to focus on only one design project at a time but have many projects each year. Other members on her team would actually implement her designs.

The designer views change as neither good nor bad— they are simply a by-product of her creative ideas. When facing a new situation or problem, the question she asks is, "Why does the idea or product work the way it does?" Risk is something to be ignored, if at all possible. The compliments a designer would most enjoy hearing are, "You are brilliant. Your brain amazes me. You were the only person to think of this solution. Your brilliant idea has really paid off well."

Not being able to think about original ideas would bring the designer the most fruestration—when the rigidity of the job and the routine of the work create certain problems and she is forced to be practical with her creative ideas. For a designer, the words she would use most often in an ideal day would be *theory, ideal, philosophy, originality, essence,* and *genius.* The point when natural energy for the job would drop is when a problem has been solved theoretically. This point could happen in a few hours in one day or take years to happen. Whenever that point is reached, the designer would want to turn over the project to someone else to make a prototype or implement the solution. The designer prefers abstract ideas and theories and would rather leave the practical details to someone else.

How a designer views or perceives others and their work styles is key to team chemistry, but often a designer will perceive another designer as a potential competitor. Designers work best together when each is assigned a different area of responsibility. A designer views a designer/developer respectfully for his ability to understand and practically apply the designer's ideas or solutions. A developer is seen as a necessary part of the work team, but daily interaction isn't considered important. The designer views a developer/stabilizer as simply too detail oriented to communicate with easily. The stabilizer is to be avoided, if at all possible, by the designer. She sees him as too controlling and not essential to her job success.

Designer/Developer

Designer/developers want to see practical application of their theoretical ideas. They want to see a prototype or solution to a problem implemented. Ideally they'll have their own original idea and the resources to make it happen. The designer/developer is happiest when he is the first to see his unique idea applied in a workable way. He is comfortable working on several major projects at the same time in various stages of design and development.

The designer/developer views change as a clear opportunity to execute his ideas. He anticipates change and takes advantage of it to create a model for a better reality. When faced with a new problem or situation, he naturally wonders about the steps to take and the order in which to take them. He develops a big-picture vision as he identifies how the macro pieces that are needed to form a holistic solution fit together. He sees risk as a reality to be lived with. He neither particularly enjoys it nor needlessly fears it.

The compliments he most enjoys receiving are, "You are wise. You can always see the big picture. Your wisdom often impacts the entire direction of our team." The designer/developer is frustrated most by situations where he cannot influence practical change. He is reluctant to trust others with his ideas or solutions and can sometimes wait too long before handing them off to the person responsible for implementation. Words he would use most often in a day sync up with his work style: *prototype, influence, process, big picture, future,* and *long-range.* The point at which there is a discernable drop off in energy is when the prototype of the original idea is eighty-five percent completed. The designer/developer is energized by the process of taking an idea from a blank sheet of paper to making it work for the first time. At that point he is ready to delegate it to someone else he trusts to further implement it.

The designer/developer must have an awareness of his work style and the work styles of others in his workplace or on his team in order to communicate effectively. He will see another designer/developer as a competitor. It is important to assign distinct projects to help them work effectively. He will view the designer with deep respect for her brilliant mind, and the developer will be seen as a great help in accomplishing the project once the model or solution has been designed and developed. He will see the developer/stabilizer as a valued member of his team, someone who is great at getting the results he expects from his model or solution. The stabilizer will be seen as an essential partner to keep the project consistent.

Developer

Developers take a model or solution that has already been designed and make it successful. The developer prefers working on someone else's great idea (why recreate the wheel?) with an existing model and a clear goal. They see making the idea a success within a given time frame as a new challenge. The developer has seen the model work initially and wants to get the project off the ground. They work on only one major project at a time, though it may have several moving parts. Once the project is up and running, or the solution has been initially implemented, they can move on to the next project.

The developer sees change as a new challenge and gets bored at work without it. When facing a new issue or challenge, they intuitively ask, "How can we get this project off the ground? What proven strategies can we adopt from somewhere or someone else?" Risk-taking is enjoyed—in fact, if no risk exists, they'll create one. Developers enjoy receiving compliments like, "You are courageous. You tackle projects that would intimidate most people. You accept a new challenge and are successful in achieving your goal."

The greatest frustration for a developer is when there are clear roadblocks that prevent them from achieving their goal. On an ideal day, they would use words such as *impact, motivate, success, goal, adapt,* and *challenge.* The developer will lose natural energy when the project has gone on for too long. The maximum time they prefer to work on a project is two years. Two years and one day is too long. An ideal project range would be three months to two years—long enough to get it going and then delegate it to someone else for refinement and maintenance.

Individuals with this work style will view other developers as potential competitors. They need to have their own project where there are no other developers on the team. They will see the designer as someone to mostly be ignored because they'll think she is too idealistic and separated from practical realities. The designer/developer is a kindred spirit who they'll see as extremely capable in most situations. The developer views the developer/stabilizer as the hand-off person—the one who can follow through on project details and clean up any loose ends. They will see the Stabilizer as detail obsessed, too focused on negatives, and lacking in vision.

Developer/Stabilizer

The developer/stabilizer sees the high potential of a project but also sees the practical problems that exist in implementation. The opportunity to take a great model and improve upon it is what the developer/stabilizer enjoys doing most. Her best work is showcased by refining already-developed ideas. The end result is the highest possible outcome. She only works on one project at a time, striving to improve, refine, and maximize it. Once that is accomplished, she can move on to the next project.

Change for a developer/stabilizer is necessary but somewhat stressful. She prefers very gradual change. In her work, the question she naturally asks about a project or solution is, "How can we maximize the situation? What can we do to improve the results? How can we eliminate the roadblocks and reach this project's full potential?" Developer/stabilizers carefully evaluate risk and believe that most risks can be avoided by doing lots of research. The compliments she appreciates the most are, "You are faithful. You make things better. You get the job done. You are most responsible for the great results we have achieved on this project."

The developer/stabilizer is most frustrated when she believes a lot of potential is being wasted—when she is moved from one project to the next before she can refine and maximize results. Loose ends and uncompleted details keep her up at night. The words she would use most often in an ideal day are *improve, refine, debug, cost effective, results,* and *maximize.* The developer/stabilizer can keep her energy level up for a fairly long time. If it takes four to five years to finally get the best results, she will do it. She likes working on a project long enough to fully develop it and get the maximum results.

Individuals with this work style will view other developer/stabilizers as potential competitors who could impact their results. In their mind, only one person can champion the improvements or refinements needed in a project. Their perception of designers is that they're impractical because their models or solutions require many tweaks to be effective. They see a designer/developer as an important generalist who sets the direction for the team or project. The developer/stabilizer views the developer as one who produces products or programs too quickly, without the necessary refinement and testing. They see the stabilizer as conservative in his approach and a bit too controlling.

Stabilizer

An ideal assignment for a stabilizer is a project that's running smoothly and needs to be kept on point. The stabilizer looks to make everything as efficient as possible so that the entire team benefits. Whereas the developer/stabilizer is more task-oriented, the stabilizer is more people-oriented. He is loyal to the team and committed to maintaining quality. He enjoys working with ideas that are practical rather than theoretical. He looks to organize, monitor efficiency, and keep things under control. He likes to work with one major project at a time, although it may have several parts to it.

The stabilizer sees change as something to be highly controlled. He is extremely uncomfortable with too much change or change happening too quickly. When he is faced with a problem or new situation, he naturally asks, "How can we get this project under control or regulate the solution? How can we keep this project running smoothly?" The stabilizer views risk as something to be avoided if at all possible. It is better to be conservative and secure rather than risky and uncertain.

The compliments he most enjoys are, "You are loyal. You are one of the most dedicated people on the team. You keep everything running well and in order. Your team always seems so devoted." He is most frustrated by situations where things are out of control and when inefficiency becomes routine or acceptable. The stabilizer is not comfortable with constantly changing plans or when procedures are forced on him. In an ideal day, the words the stabilizer loves to hear are *efficiency, prevention, maintenance, routine, predictable,* and *control.* His energy can be maintained for many years—five to as much as twenty years. Except if there is disloyalty on the team, then he will want a change.

A stabilizer views another stabilizer as a potential threat. Each stabilizer needs their own project to control. He perceives a designer as bright and creative but unrealistic and unpredictable. He sees the designer/developer as a big-picture person who can bring vision but also realism. The stabilizer will view the developer as somewhat careless and not focused enough on the details. He sees the developer/stabilizer as a vital team member and a good manager.

. . . . .

Your work is the single greatest amount of time you spend each day. Knowing your style can help you to find the greatest satisfaction in your job. The question is not "What can I do?" but "What is the best use of my time and energy?" If you are not in the right role for your style, try to move in a direction that will get you to the right one. It may mean another position on your team, it may mean another department, or it may mean a new company or organization.

You might have to experiment some to find just the right role for your work style. At some point one role will emerge as your best fit, your greatest preference, and the work you would like the most to do. In such a role, you will not only be fulfilled but you will better understand others on your team and communicate more effectively with them. When there is a new project, you will understand how you and your coworkers can contribute to achieve the greatest success. Each person can be in a position where they prefer to perform rather than feel obligated to perform.

WORK STYLES INVENTORY

- For each statement, mark to what extent it is true of your life:

  3=VERY

  2=SOME

  1=LITTLE

0=NOT AT ALL

- Put a number in the blank before each statement.

- Transfer the numbers you gave for each statement to the grid at the end of the inventory.

- Total each column. The highest number identifies your preferred work style; the next highest number, your secondary style.

1. My ideal assignment would be: Starting with a blank sheet of paper to design an absolutely new, totally unique, original idea. Coming up with a creative solution to a theoretical problem.

2. My ideal assignment would be: Starting with a blank sheet of paper to come up with my own original idea and make it practical, I'd have unlimited resources.

3. My ideal assignment would be: Making an idea extremely successful within two years.

4. My ideal assignment would be: refining a project with high potential but lots of practical problems to maximize the results.

5. My ideal assignment would be: Keeping a project that's running smoothly under control. Making it as efficient as possible so everyone benefits.

☐ 6. The point at which I "burn out" is when a problem is solved theoretically. This may take a few hours, or it may take a few years. Ideally, I would then turn it over to someone else to make a prototype and let them work out the practical details.

☐ 7. The point at which I "burn out" is when the prototype of my original idea is 85 percent done. I am energized as long as it takes to get my original "blank sheet of paper" idea working for the first time; then I will delegate it to someone I trust to develop my original idea.

☐ 8. The point at which I "burn out" is two years and one day into a project. The maximum time I prefer to work on any project is two years. I prefer a project that ranges from three months to two years—long enough to "get it going" and then delegate it to a person who will refine and maintain it.

☐ 9. The point at which I "burn out" is after about four to five years or when things are going smoothly. I like working on a project long enough to "get my teeth into it" and maximize the results.

☐ 10. The point at which I "burn out" is five to twenty years or when there is disloyalty on the team. I like things to stay the same as long as I feel we have a loyal team. When I sense a lack of loyalty, I want a change.

☐ 11. Change is neither good nor bad; it is simply a by-product of my original ideas.

☐ 12. Change is an opportunity. I anticipate change and take advantage of it.

☐ 13. Change is a new challenge. I get bored without change.

☐ 14. Change is necessary but somewhat stressful. I prefer very gradual change.

☐ 15. Change is something that must be controlled. I feel extremely uncomfortable with too much change, too fast.

☐ 16. The compliments I would most enjoy receiving would be, "You are brilliant." "Your brain is amazing." "You were the first person to think of the solution." "Your brilliant idea really paid off."

☐ 17. The compliments I would most enjoy receiving would be, "You are wise." "You see the big picture." "Your wisdom often influences our entire direction as a team."

☐ 18. The compliments I would most enjoy receiving would be, "You are courageous." "You tackle projects that intimidate most people." "You accept a challenge and are successful in achieving your goals."

19. The compliments I would most enjoy receiving would be, "You are faithful." "You get the task done." "You are a refiner and maximizer." "You are responsible for the results we have achieved in this entire project."

20. The compliments I would most enjoy receiving would be, "You are loyal." "You are one of the most loyal people on the team." "You keep things under control, running smoothly." "The group you work with always seems loyal."

21. I would be most frustrated by situations in which I am not able to think about any of my original ideas. Rigidity and routine cause nitty-gritty problems. I am forced to make my original ideas practical.

22. I would be most frustrated by situations in which I can't influence change—I have to stay with one of my new ideas too long before a follow-through person can take it over.

23. I would be most frustrated by situations in which roadblocks keep me from my goals.

24. I would be most frustrated by situations in which a lot of potential is wasted. I get moved from one project to the next before I can maximize the first one. Loose ends keep me awake at night.

☐ 25. I would be most frustrated by situations in which things are "out of control." Inefficiency is routine. Constantly changing plans or procedures are forced on me.

☐ 26. I would most enjoy creating (from a blank sheet of paper) my original ideas, concepts, and models—the more theoretical the better—regardless of practicality. I like to find original ways to unlock someone else's idea.

☐ 27. I would most enjoy seeing (from a blank sheet of paper) my original ideas applied and working in practical ways for the first time.

☐ 28. I would most enjoy taking the challenge of a great new idea I've seen work once and getting the project "off the ground."

☐ 29. I would most enjoy taking an idea that is developed but needs a lot of refining and then maximizing the results.

☐ 30. I would most enjoy working with ideas that are practical, organized, efficient. and under control.

☐ 31. I would ideally work with one design project at a time and with many projects per year. Other team members would actually implement the projects.

32. I would ideally work with seven to ten major projects or activities at a time, in various stages of design and development.

33. I would ideally work with one major project at a time (although it may have several parts), get it off the ground, and move on to the next major project.

34. I would ideally work with one major project at a time (although it may have several parts), improve, refine, and maximize it and move on.

35. I would ideally work with one major project (although it may have several parts) with everything under control.

36. When facing a new situation or problem, the questions I ask naturally are, "Why does the idea or product work the way it does? What original approach will solve the problem or eliminate this situation creatively?"

37. When facing a new situation or problem, the questions I ask naturally are, "What steps should we take next? Why? How do all of the pieces fit together into a whole? What is the big picture?"

38. When facing a new situation or problem, the questions I ask naturally are, "How can we get this project "off the ground"? What proven ideas can we adapt from something or someone else?"

☐ 39. When facing a new situation or problem, the questions I ask naturally are, "How can we maximize the situation? How can we eliminate the roadblocks and reach this project's full potential? How can we improve the results?"

☐ 40. When facing a new situation or problem, the questions I ask naturally are, "How can we get this project under control? How can we keep this project running smoothly?"

☐ 41. Risk is something to be ignored, if possible.

☐ 42. Risk is something to be lived with. It is something I neither enjoy nor avoid; it's just reality.

☐ 43. Risk is something to be enjoyed. If no risk exists, I'll create one.

☐ 44. Risk is something to be carefully evaluated. I can avoid most risks by doing lots of homework.

☐ 45. Risk is something to be avoided, if possible. It is better to be conservative and safe than risky and constantly "out on a limb."

☐ 46. The words I would use most often in my ideal day would be *originality, genius, essence, ideal, theory,* and *philosophy.*

☐ 47. The words I would use most often in my ideal day would be *influence, process, future, big picture, long range*, and *prototype*.

☐ 48. The words I would use most often in my ideal day would be *challenge, goal, adapt, success, motivate*, and *impact*.

☐ 49. The words I would use most often in my ideal day would be *results, refine, maximize, improve, cost effective*, and *debug*.

☐ 50. The words I would use most often in my ideal day would be *control, efficiency, predictable, prevention, maintenance*, and *routine*.

1.	2.	3.	4.	5.
6.	7.	8.	9.	10.
11.	12.	13.	14.	15.
16.	17.	18.	19.	20.
21.	22.	23.	24.	25.
26.	26.	28.	29.	30
31.	.	33.	34.	35.
36.	37.	38.	39.	40.
41.	42.	43.	44.	45.
46.	47.	48.	49.	50.
Total	Total	Total	Total	Total
Designer	Designer/ Developer	Developer	Developer/ stabilizer	Stabilizer

CHAPTER SIX

TIME STYLES

P eople are different. For instance, I am one of those individuals who tries to get every last drop from a tube of toothpaste or a bottle of shampoo. It brings me great joy to not waste any portion of a product. There are others, though, who feel it is too much work to extract every last drop of their tube or bottle. They simply toss it in the garbage when it's almost completely empty and purchase another. This is just one example of how people approach things differently.

God has created us unique in so many ways. We have different personalities, different ethnicities, and different genders. These differences influence our opinions about many things. Toilet paper has the population almost evenly divided. People get annoyed over the toilet paper being rolled the wrong way. This is just one of the fascinating differences that Bernice Kanner reveals about Americans in her book *Are You Normal?* (Kanner 1995) She found that 53 percent of the population believes the right way to roll toilet paper is over the top. Forty-seven percent consider underneath the best way to put toilet paper on the roll.

People have different opinions about where to sit on an airplane. Fifty-seven percent prefer the window seat, while only 18 percent of the population like the aisle (as I do). People are different in how they eat corn. Fifty-eight percent of the population eats it in a row, and 42 percent eat it in a rotational pattern. When it comes to bed-making routines, Kanner found that 79 percent of the population do not even spend time doing it. Most of us have messy beds—approximately eight out of ten.

These differences certainly apply to time as well. Everyone does not view time the same way. In fact, even how they set their watches is different. When asked if they set their watch at exactly the right time or five minutes ahead, 34 percent of people said they set their watch five minutes early, 32 percent set them on time, and I guess the rest don't wear watches.

It is crucial to have a clear understanding of how our view of time impacts our lives. People see time differently particularly in relationships, and it is important to recognize the impact. We may gravitate toward others who value time in the same manner we do. Understanding these different styles can help us enormously in how we use our time and prevent us from having ongoing and consistent conflicts with others over time.

Two Ways to View Time

You can relate to time in two ways: either objectively or subjectively. If you are objective in your view of time, you are on time. If a church service starts at 10:45, you are there at or before 10:45. Conversely, when you are an individual with a subjective stance on time, arriving around 11-ish for the service is acceptable to you. You will either identify with one or the other of these ways of relating to time. You are either generally on time and are bothered when you are delayed, or you are customarily not on time and are not perturbed when that happens.

You must then evaluate which moments in time get most of your attention. Again, there are two ways to classify your response. You can categorize your attention in terms of the present or in terms of the future. If you are present-oriented, you focus on the here and now. If you are future-oriented, you focus on the "there and then." You can identify as one or the other, and this perception impacts how you relate to time, how you use your time, and how you interact with people who do not share the same time focus.

Once you identify whether you are objective or subjective about time and whether you are present-oriented or future-oriented, you can now identify your unique time style. Dr. Les Parrott categorizes people into four time styles: the accommodator, the dreamer, the planner, and the processor (Parrott 2006).

While there are four main styles for viewing time, understand that no one is 100 percent in one particular category. But you will find that you identify the most with one particular style. You may find yourself occasionally taking on characteristics of another style based on life experiences or seasons of your life, which can impact how you function with time. Yet, despite occasional changes, you will find you primarily and consistently fall into one of the four time styles. This is how you most consistently relate to time.

For those of you who are married or in significant relationships, you should understand that your time style is probably different than that of your partner. Opposites do attract. While it is rare to find two individuals who are complete opposites, there is a freshness and vitality that comes from being opposite in some areas, such as your personalities or time styles.

My wife, for instance, is an accommodator (future-oriented, living with vision) and I am a planner (present-oriented, living in the now). When I say nine o'clock, I mean nine o'clock. When my wife says nine o'clock, she means 9-ish. This seems small, but it can be a noticeable difference, especially over a long period of time. For years I tried to figure out why she could not sync up with my understanding of time. When I say it takes twenty minutes to drive to a destination, I mean twenty minutes. Conversely, my wife rounds it up or down. She might say it will take half an hour. From my objective thinking, half an hour is ten more minutes than twenty minutes or 33 percent more. Clearly, it is important to understand and identify not only your own time style but the time styles of those with whom you are constantly interacting, be it spouses, parents, friends, or coworkers.

By analyzing the time styles of those around you, you will find the source of some of your conflict and frustration. We can naturally become annoyed when people always show up late or cannot deviate from a plan to stop for a burger. Understanding time styles will help with some of that frustration. It cannot solve all of your conflicts, as each style has strengths and weaknesses. However, the goal is to help identify how you relate to time, can build on those strengths, and also work on those weaknesses that might be holding you back in your life, especially as we understand time as a precious resource.

So whatever time style you are, you need to understand how you can maximize your time and how you can use it to the best of your ability within the way God has created and wired you. What we do with our time here on earth impacts eternity. Therefore, it is so important that we use time wisely and that we value this precious resource that we have.

Not only should you identify your time style, but you should also work on your weaknesses. You have to work on those ways you relate to time that can hold you back from being all God has created you to be. You would not want to find yourself at the end of your life without having fully maximized your God-given potential because you failed to use your time well within the style and the way God has designed you. To do that, we need to examine these four styles in depth to see if we might find practical ways we can better utilize time, which would allow us to reach our full potential in God.

Accommodator

An accommodator is someone who subjectively views time from a present perspective. They are both subjective and present-oriented. In other words, these are the people who try to accommodate or adapt their schedule for whatever they want to do at a particular time. These people live in the moment. They want to be free to adjust how they use their time, which impacts their relationships when dealing with time issues. They may stop randomly at an ice cream shop because they are craving a hot fudge sundae, even though they are supposed to be headed to meet people. It is not uncommon nor a big deal for them to add or subtract detours in their daily routines.

The accommodator has many positive attributes and is someone who makes time for people. Not every time style is so obliging toward others, but individuals with this particular time style will always make time for people who need it. Moreover, accommodators will be fully present. They give "the present of presence" to other people in their lives. To help you understand what this means, consider an individual in our church who gave his spouse twelve cards, each with a message for how, on a specific day and time each month, they would spend quality time in a particular way. This person recognized that our time is one of the greatest gifts we have to give.

Accommodators do not need a particular reason or special occasion, like Christmas, to give the gift of their time. They are there for you, and they will make time for you. However, in making time for you, someone else might be hurt. You could be at the receiving end of either the blessing of unplanned presence or the loss of it. This is essentially how it works with accommodators.

For accommodators to be more wise and effective with their time, they must first set boundaries. Boundaries and accommodators do not work too well together, but they can work better. Accommodators must be better about creating limits for how obliging they will be with their time. In other words, they might decide to not allow people to impinge on their family time by refusing to respond to every phone call, text, or email during a family vacation. If you are an accommodator, you need to set certain boundaries, because without them, you are going to end up all over the place. Moreover, without boundaries, you will constantly try to adapt and adjust your schedule for people, which might end up hurting or slighting the other people in your life. While you might be tempted to deny purposefully offending anyone, you must also recognize that your decisions about time can have unintended, hurtful consequences. The goal is to improve your weakness, so recognize that boundaries are necessary for everyone, and as an accommodator this is often an area of weakness.

Another area accommodators can develop is their organizational skills. If they can be more structured and ordered, they can follow through better. Typically, an accommodator is somewhat scattered. They may be over here, then over there, working on various projects simultaneously or switching partway through. They are constantly moving and not necessarily reaching the end result. They have a tendency to have many unfinished projects. Similarly, though they are attempting to help many people, they may end up letting people down because they are not organized and thus unable to complete what they had hoped to do. In general, control is necessary; accommodators need more boundaries and organization.

Dreamer

Similar to the accommodator, dreamers are subjective about time; however, they differ in that they are future-oriented as opposed to being present-oriented. Dreamers live and think about time in terms of what could be. If you are a dreamer, your relationship with time involves future consideration and you are likely wrapped up in what is about to happen. You are constantly envisioning, contemplating, and focusing on what you hope will happen. It is important to understand this about dreamers: they focus on what they "hope" will happen.

It's necessary to understand that dreamers are very optimistic people. They are fun to be around and they are fun with their time. You may already envision who the dreamers are in your life. They randomly suggest going skydiving or snowboarding. They get a free day off and decide to drive to the beach. There is rarely a plan in place, but there is a need to act.

This way of thinking can be fun at times. Being sporadic and unpredictable can break the everyday routine and leave you with amazing memories. At the same time, dreamers need to be more realistic about life. There are sometimes responsibilities that are overlooked because dreamers are seeking adventure. There needs to be some realism put into these "fun" activities. There may be consequences for an action, and dreamers need to understand that.

One way dreamers can improve is by working on not changing plans at the last minute. Oftentimes, they "go with the flow," and then when they change the plan, they have actually jumbled up future plans. When you do not use time well in a relationship with other people and you change plans on them, you can wreck someone else's plans, which can have a very negative impact.

Not only should dreamers think through their plans, but they should also work on their response to stress.

When dreamers are stressed, they tend to be immobilized. Their inclination is to stop because their predisposition is to have fun and enjoy life. If you are a dreamer, you must work on your ability to deal with the less enjoyable aspects of life. After all, stress is also a part of life and you cannot come to a standstill when every difficulty arises. Doing so prohibits you from using your time well and hinders you in your relationships with other people.

Planner

If you are a planner, you are objective in how you look at time and future-oriented in how you spend your time. In other words, planners have a vision and they have a plan. The key thing to understand about planners is that they try to control time. That is their great focus in life, controlling how time is best utilized. Like dreamers, they see a vision for the future; they see how things could be. Unlike dreamers, they have a plan for how this will take place.

Planners are very efficient and prepared people. They are the kind of people who take action with time. They run this world. They are the people that get stuff done. They have a vision, make a plan, and follow through with it. They value time greatly and seek to use their time in the most effective way possible.

While we all benefit from having planners in our lives, they need to learn how to live more fully in the moment. Planners are focused on the future and making the necessary preparations. They are so absorbed in what could happen and how to make their vision a reality that they often do not stop to smell the roses.

Another area for planners to evaluate is their ability to multitask. While this often means they can accomplish a lot of different tasks at once, they are also not necessarily fully focused in a particular moment or on a particular person. Planners need to work on patience, especially as it relates to stressful situations. Planners can sometimes be inundated with stress when people are not doing what they are supposed to be doing. Planners want everyone to line up and contribute with their assigned task, and they have a difficult time understanding why people do not move in the same manner or pace as they do.

Planners have to work on their patience because time is so valuable to them. They feel every moment matters, and to lose time or waste it is unacceptable to them. But since individuals cannot always control the pace at which others move, planners need to be more empathetic and understanding of people's different time styles. Being impatient can be hurtful, and this lack of patience can come across as a lack of caring or sensitivity.

Processor

The processer is also objective in terms of time, but his is also present-oriented. In other words, processors are structured in their time and travel at a definitive pace. They, like planners, prefer schedules, but unlike planners, they do not like to surmise about possible future events. They base their decisions solely on the here and now.

Processers are very punctual people and are very disciplined with their time. They are very helpful because they keep all of us on schedule. Processors are rarely if ever late. While timeliness is important, processors can also be too rigid with their time, unable to change. They can become so enraptured with their schedule that they become flustered with the idea that the schedule might need to change. Even if the change can be proven to be necessary or proven to be valuable, they are distressed by the need to make a time change.

Processors need to adjust what happens to them while they experience stress. Many can become compulsive, which is a psychological term. A spiritual term would be legalistic. In other words, they refuse to budge, believing things must stay the way they are, even if it is not for the best. This sort of compulsion prevents one from seeing the possibility of doing things differently or altering some parts of the schedule. One such example is a kindergarten teacher whose students ran back and forth across the open space in her room. She would constantly scold the children, telling them that they should not run back and forth. Every day this happened, and every day she would become more stressed. She could not believe they would not follow her very simple rule. Another teacher walked in and saw the teacher distressed. It was obvious this had been a long battle. He noted that she refused to believe that there was anything else she could do. However, he saw another option. He rearranged her classroom so that the open space to run back and forth no longer existed. That small adjustment was all that was needed. Now it was impossible for the students to run back and forth. She could not see this possibility because she refused to believe that there was another option. The students just needed to learn to not run. Being open to hearing and seeing alternative plans and ideas can make life less stressful. Believing that the way you have always used time is the only way will cause you to face unnecessary difficulties. Be open to the possibility of different schedules.

. . . . .

Regardless of your time style, you will find, as in other aspects of your life, that there are both strengths and weaknesses. When you build on your strengths, you can really use time wisely in the way in which God has created you. More importantly, you'll understand that you cannot choose these characteristics about yourself. This is the time style God created for you.

That's why it's important to understand that God has created us and equipped us differently. We need to work on those aspects of our lives that are weaknesses, especially as it relates to time and relationships. We need to use time in the best possible way, as the Bible encourages us, within the way in which God has uniquely designed us, so we can fulfill our purpose on this earth.

And we need to become more understanding and accepting of people's differences as we develop relationships. By working on our own weaknesses, building on our strengths, and becoming more understanding about the different time styles people have, we can end up using this precious resource of time very well.

TIME STYLES INVENTORY

- For each statement, mark to what extent it is true of your life:

  3=VERY

2=SOME

1=LITTLE

0=NOT AT ALL

- Put a number in the blank before each statement.

- Transfer the numbers you gave for each statement to the grid at the end of the inventory.

- Total each column. The highest number identifies your preferred time style; the next highest number, your secondary style.

☐ 1. I always make time for people who need it.

☐ 2. I am optimistic and like having fun.

☐ 3. I like to be prepared, which helps me get things done.

☐ 4. I am disciplined with my time and am rarely late.

☐ 5. I like to do similar activities all the time.

☐ 6. Sometimes acting on impulse makes me miss important obligations I already have scheduled.

☐ 7. Time is valuable to me, and I like to use it in the most effective way possible.

☐ 8. I may become distressed by the need to make a time change.

☐ 9. I find I need to set boundaries; otherwise I can be too accommodating for some which may hurt others.

☐ 10. Since I like to "go with the flow," I may mess up other peoples' plans.

☐ 11. Because I like to plan for the future, I may miss some of the good things happening in the present.

☐ 12. I think schedules must stay the same, even if change is necessary or possibly more valuable.

☐ 13. Sometimes I am scattered and find it hard to reach a goal.

☐ 14. I find that stress can be immobilizing because I have a hard time dealing with less enjoyable aspects of life.

☐ 15. I am impatient when it comes to the pace that others work at, which sometimes makes others feel that I don't care or lack sensitivity.

☐ 16. When I'm stressed, I am often compulsive and cannot see the advantage to changing the schedule or doing things differently.

1.	2.	3.	4.
5.	6.	7.	8.
9.	10	11	12
13.	14.	15.	16.
Total	Total	Total	Total
Accommodator	**Dreamer**	**Planner**	**Processor**

CHAPTER SEVEN

LEARNING STYLES

E ach of us learns in our own way, and there is a reason why you learn more easily in certain situations than in others. Understanding your learning style helps you make sense of past learning experiences and helps you get the most out of future learning opportunities. A learning style is the way you perceive or see information and then use or process what you have learned.

Your learning style has nothing to do with achievement level, IQ, or socioeconomic background. But when you can learn in your preferred style, you are more likely to succeed to your full potential. Your learning style holds clues about how to develop your natural abilities to their highest level.

Knowing your learning style can dramatically change your opinion of yourself. Likewise, your children, spouse, and coworkers can also benefit from understanding their leaning styles. Too many people have thought they are dumb, have nothing of value to offer, or are destined to mediocrity. They may have even dropped out of school or given up on their dreams. In reality, they simply did not learn in the same way as everyone else and suffered as a result.

Effective learning follows a certain natural process. Learning does not take place in a vacuum. What we already know provides the foundation for what we will learn. This connection prepares us to learn something new. As we learn new content, we practice how it actually works in our lives. Then we take what we have learned and definitively apply it.

Evaluating what you hear, see, and experience is complex. Past preferences, biases, skills, and other factors impact how you learn. But this process does follow a consistent path. In order to learn anything, you need to eliminate distractions and anything that limits your ability to assimilate information. This will allow you to give your full attention to learning. You then need to make sense of the new information in such a way that it matches with your concepts of the way things work or with your existing knowledge. This may first mean unlearning something so new learning can happen. The next step is relating new information with existing patterns or knowledge in your short- or long-term memory. This connects new information with what you already know. Finally, new information is comprehended, and your new knowledge can be used.

This learning cycle can happen in a few seconds or take much longer, especially if new information is confusing or complex. When this cycle is successfully completed, you will likely feel positive and ready to apply what you have learned. If you experience difficulties with one of the steps, you may feel negative or confused.

Understanding your learning style will help you identify where you may encounter challenges along your learning path.

Knowing your learning style can also give you a much more positive attitude about learning. Once you find the way that you learn best, you can seek out learning regardless of the obstacles in your way. Ideally you have a desire to know something new or have a need in your life that requires new knowledge. Certainly an immediate need will motivate you to learn. You may need to manage change or a transition. You may want to increase your self-esteem or success. In the end, there must be an intrinsic curiosity or interest for you to learn.

Jay Zagorsky, a professor at Ohio State University, has done research on income and wealth as it relates to intelligence. His study "Do You Have To Be Smart To Be Rich?" (Zagorsky 2007) concluded that someone of average or even below-average intelligence is capable of accumulating as much or more wealth than someone who is extremely intelligent. He wrote, "During the course of a lifetime, those of average intelligence can accumulate a lot of wealth through wise investments and other methods by learning through various means." In other words, a positive learning stance about finances is more important than your IQ for gaining wealth and financial security.

Your learning motivation is impacted by your previous experiences. By discovering your learning style, you can have a new perspective on how you learn. Of course, if the content is of no interest to you, it is unlikely you will have the necessary motivation. If you don't believe you need to learn, it is not a priority for you, or the subject has no real attraction, any motivation is unlikely. But learning also involves persistence and concentration. You need to be aware of your own levels of concentration and persistence in learning new material. Also, knowing whether you like to study on your own (like online education) or whether you need live instruction is crucial.

Almost forty years ago, Bernice McCarthy developed the 4MAT System where she identified four distinct learning styles (McCarthy 1987). Everyone does not learn the same way. God has made your mind right, and God can use your unique intelligence. Identifying your learning style can change your opinion of yourself and what you are willing to attempt for Jesus.

But before we look at the four learning styles we need to establish your approach to learning. There are two distinct ways.

Telescopic Approach

People tend to be at one end of the spectrum or the other in terms of a context for learning. On one end are those who are telescopic. They are able to focus on the core teaching without being distracted. If you are telescopic, you can analyze individual elements of the information you receive. You are analytical. Your focus on details is your strength, but it can cause you to miss the larger point or the application of it.

Telescopic learners have high concentration when there is a clear link with their personal goals, but their engagement with the lesson can be low if there is too much time spent on other material unrelated to the core teaching. They prefer learning goals, objectives, and a clear message on how to reach them. Motivation is self-generated and quickly developed but can disappear if they are not challenged. They will adjust to their learning environment wherever possible and ignore minor distractions. Any learning format is fine as long as the teacher can be seen and they can hear clearly.

Telescopic learners approach learning in an analytical way. They like step-by-step instruction, pay close attention to details, and need to know the teacher's expectations. Having opinions expressed as facts, not understanding the purpose of an assignment, and dealing in generalities frustrates them. They want to finish one task before moving on to another and do not need to find meaning in all they learn. Organization, details, consistency, and objectivity are their learning strengths.

Wide-Angled Approach

On the other end of the contextual spectrum are those who are wide-angled. If this is your approach, you may tend to notice all aspects of the learning environment. This is your strength but it may cause you to be easily frustrated by distractions when you are trying to focus. Environmental factors like light, noise, or other physical influences can interfere with your learning.

Wide-angled learners concentrate best when the learning environment provides for all learning styles. They prefer various ways of teaching and learning. Learning goals and objectives need to be explained from the start. Motivation is created when there is a proper learning environment, not just a focus on content. They are likely to be distracted by even minor noises or interruptions. A room that has an attractive design with lots of light is an optimal learning climate.

Wide-angled learners approach learning in a conceptual way. They learn by discussion and working with others. Being sensitive to others' feelings, being flexible, and being future-focused are some of their personal qualities. But in going with the flow and avoiding conflict, they may skip needed steps and details. They need to understand the purpose for their learning and be able to relate it to their situation. Their strengths are in seeing the big picture, valuing group learning, getting others involved, and understanding various options in learning.

Once you have identified your approach to learning you can now find out which learning style fits you.

Imaginative Style

Imaginative learners favor feeling and reflecting. They tend to ask themselves, "Why do I need to know this?" They learn best in environments where interpersonal relationships are developed. Because they are comfortable with their feelings and are people-oriented, learning through questions, listening, and sharing ideas is what they enjoy. The imaginative student is an outstanding observer of people and is committed to making the world a better place.

They see the big picture or broad overview more than the small details. They can see all sides of issues being presented. This style is all about talking, listening, watching, responding, asking questions, brainstorming, and examining all viewpoints. Imaginative learners work well in groups but can also enjoy reading quietly.

They have difficulty giving oral presentations, memorizing large amounts of abstract information, and with long verbal explanations. They dislike settings where mistakes are openly criticized, where they cannot discuss their perceptions, and where there is conflict or confusion. This style puts perception before judgment, reflection before action, and subjective knowledge before objective fact. These learners prefer to make decisions based on feeling and are experiential rather than conceptual.

An imaginative learner may be underappreciated and underutilized. They can be very helpful in closing the "back door" of a church where people leave because they feel the church isn't friendly. Their ministry of welcoming and talking with people makes them feel more connected. When there is conflict, they can keep people together and bring about harmony.

They use their life experience as a foundation for gaining new knowledge. They think in paragraphs more than in sentences. The more they talk, the greater their knowledge becomes. Many classroom settings do not favor this style of learning. This learner needs to talk and interact. They are a people person—they see facts in terms of people. They want to know how much you care before they care how much you know. Imaginative learners can disrupt the class with constant talking or monopolize a conversation. They may depend too much on others for their identity and what they think of them.

It should be obvious that the learning style of a teacher will dictate their teaching style. Their definition of success will be influenced by their style. For example, an imaginative style youth pastor will view success in his

ministry as the kids learning to know God and themselves. He would want them to care for one another and
be honest and open with each other. He would want to be
seen as a caring person who wants good things to happen
in their lives.

Analytic Style

Analytical learners favor thinking and reflecting. They
tend to ask themselves, "What do I need to know?" They
learn by listening and watching. They expect the teacher
to be the primary source of information while they listen and evaluate the value of the information presented. These are the students who best learn the way most
teaching has traditionally been done, and thus they are
likely considered the best learners. They want to get all
A's, all the right answers in school and in their lives.

These learners have a knowledge-oriented style; they
analyze and classify ideas and experiences, are excellent
at conceptualizing material, are highly organized, and
are comfortable with data and details. They are good at
step-by-step tasks, believe in their intellectual ability, are
attracted to structure, and are committed to making the
world understandable.

Analytic learners are uncomfortable in an unfamil-
iar learning environment. They want facts and objective
explanations delivered through lectures. These learners
can work independently and systematically, but only
with clear direction. They will have difficulty working in
groups, in noisy or high-activity environments, and in ambiguous situations. They will also have trouble with role-
playing, open-ended assignments, oral presentations, and

non-sequential instructions. They experience difficulty talking about their feelings as well.

They value facts and figures, smart and wise people, and being right. Analytic learners are curious about ideas—they enjoy taking notes, define themselves by how smart they are, and see themselves as intellectual. These learners are highly competitive, think in terms of right and wrong answers, and dislike methods where there is not a clear winner.

This style is the one most parents would like their children to have. Teachers love analytic learners because analytic learners love teachers. They listen, follow directions, and love to find the right answers. Most people will think they are smart even though geniuses exist in every learning style. They often achieve high grades and a top college education. Their rational thinking is rewarded in highly regarded fields like medicine and law.

Analytic learners rely more on thinking than feelings in making right decisions. Their thought processes tend to be only about what is rational, logical, critical and generally impersonal. They will research Christianity before accepting Christ as their Savior. They will read the Bible, read Christian books, and evaluate the gospel message, seeking out all the facts before making a decision. Only after rational thought and reasoning will they likely consider taking a step of faith.

Because they are more knowledge-oriented than people-oriented, those with an analytic learning style can appear to be picky, superior, and demanding. They have little tolerance for the sharing of more feeling-generated ideas and are not encumbered with self-doubt.

For example, an analytic style youth pastor will view success in his ministry by his students' love for studying solid biblical content and participating in in-depth discussions. He would have a highly disciplined structure, and the youth would see him as a Bible scholar. He would know he succeeded when his students were prepared to give an answer to anyone who would ask them what they believe and why.

Common-Sense Style

Common-sense learners favor thinking and doing. They tend to ask themselves, "How does this work?" They like to work with ideas and see if they are rational and workable. These learners want to test out theories in the real world and put into practice what they have learned. They are hands-on; they use their own ideas, evaluate problems, and then solve them. They love to get the job done. Common-sense learners excel when dealing with what is practical and of immediate importance to them. They simply learn best when learning is combined with doing.

They are great problem solvers drawn to understand how things work. They believe in their ability to get a task accomplished or meet a deadline. They are active and need opportunities to move around. These learners are very productive and are committed to making the world a better place. They prefer to learn through active problem solving: manipulating, constructing, and step-by-step procedures. They enjoy demonstrations, experimentation, and competition.

Common-sense learners have difficulty when reading is the primary way of learning and they have no opportunity to test out what they have been taught. They have trouble with paradoxes or ambiguous choices, verbal complexity, and open-ended academic tasks. And they are not good with expressing feelings and subtle relationships. This style is about facts before ideas, action before reflection, and judgment before perception.

They value strategic thinking above philosophical thinking. Action and doing are their strategies for learning. They think about problems logically, break them down into parts, and then pieces, and then develop a workable solution. They are motivated by how to make something useful. These learners want to connect everything they learn to the moment. They live in the here and now. Everything must make sense to them immediately, if they see no conceivable use for the information, they may dismiss it as unimportant.

These learners also need to move as part of the learning process. Testing requires action—it can't simply be done in their heads. Their minds cannot be fully activated if their hands or another part of their body is not moving. This is why some boys have such struggles in traditional classroom settings. These are some of the same boys who break a toy so they can take it apart to see how it works. They strive to make things work, to make things right. They may be more concerned about logical consequences than personal feelings.

In the church they become champions of compassion ministry. They are interested in seeing the practical impact the Christian faith can make in people's lives. Serving in the homeless ministry, mentoring at-risk kids, and volunteering at the food pantry all make sense to them as ways to live out the Christian life.

Relationships may suffer as they strive to make projects work and meet deadlines. They can come across as pushy, harsh, or even dominating because they will do anything to get the job done.

A common-sense youth pastor would see success in his ministry when the youth are enjoying projects where they show their faith in action. He would want them to test if what he has taught them is true. The youth would be given an important job to do, and then he would step back and allow them to do it successfully.

Dynamic Style

Dynamic learners favor creating and acting. They tend to ask themselves, "What can this become?" They want action in the learning process, but rather than thinking rationally about a project and the steps to take, they want to follow hunches for new directions or possibilities. They are risk-takers who love to start something new from information they have learned or even an existing idea or project they've put their own original spin on. Flexibility and being change friendly are their hallmarks. When they learn something new, they get excited and come up with an array of ideas for moving forward.

As Christ followers they will champion a new ministry. They will help the people of their church see what a great idea it is. They will also have the courage to take a stand and ask others to stand with them. If they believe in a group or event, they will get behind it, wholeheartedly sacrificing their time and money to see it be successful.

They are comfortable with ambiguity, are proud of their subjectivity, and are willing to take risks. They want to enrich their learning experience by extending it beyond traditional methods. Instead of writing a report on juvenile justice, a dynamic learner would visit the juvenile court herself and present it as a skit instead of a written report. These learners challenge boundaries for the sake of growth and change, and they believe in their ability to influence their world. They are entrepreneurs. They look for unique aspects in the information they learn, and they continue to learn through trial and error.

This style likes to learn through talking, convincing, self-discovery, and finding creative solutions to problems. They engage in a free flight of ideas and are willing to work independently. Because their interpersonal skills are so good, they embrace open-ended learning tasks with lots of options, paradox, and subtle relationships. They have difficulty with fixed routines where they are not allowed to question them. Also, they have trouble with methodical tasks, visual complexity, time management, and absolutes.

Dynamic learners view everything with a future orientation. They enjoy ideas and consider learning fun because of the variety. Flexibility defines them. They do not have to see a project through from idea to implementation. They may have ten ideas when everyone else has one. Ideas come so naturally to them that they may value good ideas more than a fully developed plan. They can enjoy each new idea so much that they lose interest in the old ones.

This style of learner is willing to go it alone, to take a risk with little fear of failure. They can challenge the teacher by wanting to do something totally different, and they can often be heard saying "but." Dynamic learners are intuitive and value creative expression. They are often leaders because of their ideas and their enthusiasm. But they can be egotistical. They may have difficulty acknowledging the contribution of those who think more traditionally or analytically. As leaders they have to guard against being manipulative and undisciplined.

The dynamic youth pastor would view success in his ministry when the youth are involved in their faith—when they see hurting people and are active in finding new ways to minister to them. He would be the catalyst for their actions.

. . . . .

Knowing about learning styles can help understand our family dynamics. Over 80 percent of us marry our opposite learning style. Imaginative and common-sense learners are opposite. So are analytic and dynamic. We are attracted to people who intrigue us with their differences. Then we get married and have children with different learning styles.

A great date idea for an imaginative would be to throw a party. An analytic would go to a documentary or art film. A common-sense would go bowling. A dynamic would go skydiving. The reaction to the news about having their first baby would differ greatly. An imaginative would call all her friends and family and tell them the good news. An analytic would start researching books on parenting. A common-sense would start building a cradle. A dynamic would sign up the baby for sports programs and music classes. And in picking a church to attend, the most important consideration would vary widely too. An imaginative would look for the friendliest church. An an-alytic would look for sound theology. A common-sense would look for opportunities to serve. A dynamic would look for a cutting-edge ministry.

By affirming your learning style, you accept your pre-ferred way of learning. This results in many positive out-comes. You truly believe God has made your mind right. You recognize your personal talents that can be used to serve God and others. You are more motivated to keep learning new things. You now understand others better (your spouse, children, coworkers, and friends) and can be more tolerant and accepting. And you can relate better in various group situations.

LEARNING STYLES INVENTORY

- For each statement, mark to what extent it is true of your life:

  3=VERY

  2=SOME

  1=LITTLE

  0=NOT AT ALL

- Put a number in the blank before each statement.

- Transfer the numbers you gave for each statement to the grid at the end of the inventory.

- Total each column. The highest number identifies your preferred learning style; the next highest number, your secondary style.

☐ 1. I am hands-on, using my own ideas, evaluating problems, and then solving them.

☐ 2. I like to solve problems by making guesses or following hunches.

☐ 3. I prefer learning goals, objectives, and a clear message on how to reach them.

☐ 4. Goals and objectives need to be explained to me from the start.

☐ 5. I have to know how things work.

☐ 6. I am a risk-taker and love to start something new by putting an original spin on an existing idea or project.

☐ 7. I am able to focus without being distracted.

☐ 8. I can be easily distracted by noises and interruptions.

☐ 9. I am competitive and enjoy demonstrations and experiments.

☐ 10. I like to brainstorm new ideas and try things not many people would dare to try.

☐ 11. I like step-by-step instructions.

☐ 12. I learn best in a room that has an attractive design and lots of light.

☐ 13. I have trouble expressing my feelings.

☐ 14. I like playing with new ideas, making intuitive guesses on what works.

☐ 15. To me it's "just the facts." I don't like generalities.

☐ 16. I learn best by discussion and working with others.

☐ 17. People may think I'm pushy, harsh or even dominating because I will do anything to "get the job done."

☐ 18. I am willing to go it alone with little fear of failure.

☐ 19. I am organized, detail oriented, consistent, and objective.

☐ 20. It's easy for me to see the big picture.

☐ 21. My learning motto is "Why do I need to know this?"

☐ 22. My learning motto is "What do I need to know?"

☐ 23. My learning motto is "How does this work?"

[ ] 24. My learning motto is "What can this become?"

1.	2.	3.	4.
5.	6.	7.	8.
9.	10	11	12
13.	14.	15.	16.
17.	18.	19.	20.
21.	22.	23.	24.
Total	Total	Total	Total
Imaginative	Analytic	Common-Sense	Dynamic

CHAPTER EIGHT

LEADERSHIP STYLES

I had an opportunity to visit Gettysburg, Pennsylvania, on a trip. You could hardly visit a place that is a bigger leadership lab than Gettysburg. Gettysburg is the site of the single biggest battles in American history. Fifty thousand men lost their lives over three days. There is nothing like it, in sheer numbers, compared to any battle in any war America has ever fought. Every other just pales in comparison to what took place at Gettysburg.

So much of what happened there is all about leadership; what went right, what went wrong. General Lee went to Gettysburg believing that if he could win on Northern soil, the war could be over. He actually had a letter with him from the Confederate president Jefferson Davis to give to President Lincoln, essentially saying, "We've won a number of battles in a row. We've won on your soil. Let's just call it a tie. We will cease fighting and we'll each just go our own way."

The Union General Reynolds, knowing the fight was coming, grabbed the high ground. And even though he was killed within the first half hour of battle on the first day, his decision to occupy the high ground was ultimately why the Union forces succeeded. There were many other factors, but it is not an oversimplification that this was the key to victory over the Confederate forces. Joshua Chamberlain, who was a college professor in Maine, was in no way a warrior. Most of the leaders who fought at Gettysburg were not professional soldiers. Some were West Point trained, some were Virginia Military Institute trained, but most were just regular people. Chamberlain's leadership was enormously important and significant. In fact, he received the Congressional Medal of Honor.

Maybe the most powerful leadership lesson of all that came out of Gettysburg was that after Pickett's charge failed and the Union really had the upper hand, General Meade did not pursue Lee. If he had pursued him, it is possible he could have overcome Lee. And if he had, it would have effectively ended the Civil War. The war would have been over if the top Confederate force, the Army of Northern Virginia, led by General Lee, had been defeated. But General Meade chose not to attack the retreating confederates. And because he chose not to, the war went on for two more years, and thousands more lives were lost.

Leadership is a big deal. Leadership makes companies successes or failures. Leadership makes families fall apart or last. Leadership causes teams to win or lose. Leadership causes churches to grow or to maintain or even fail. Leadership is enormously significant. Leadership is influence. Every time you influence people or influence a situation, you assume leadership. Leadership is influence.

When I was younger, my father used to say to me, "Rick, you are a natural born leader," which didn't mean much to me at the time. I didn't really know what it meant. I always had leadership positions in school and on teams. As I went to college, I continued to be a leader. But at some point I realized I needed to learn about leadership. I took a class in college called "Leadership and Organizational Development" taught by a retired Army colonel, and I loved it. It advanced my leadership acumen, but I had much more to learn.

I started reading a lot of leadership books, and most of what I read was business related. Many of the books were written by professors at business schools. Then I came across John Maxwell. He was the first person I'd read who talked about leadership from a church perspective. I devoured just about everything he wrote. I visited with him in conferences and meetings because I wanted to learn more about leadership. He stressed that nothing of consequence happens with groups of people without leadership. I became convinced that leadership, more than any other skill, was the key to organizational success.

Leadership is needed in all kinds of places in our world. Some believe they are not a leader because they are not the president of this or the director of that or have never been elected to an office. There is much more to leadership than just a few positions or titles. Leadership can occur in an informal way. You don't have to have prestigious certifications behind your name or in front of it to be a leader. You can lead right where you are—in your school, in the workplace, in the home, in your neighborhood—wherever it might be.

I am passionate about the fact that this world could be a better place, our nation could be a better place, our community could be a better place, your home could be a better place, and the church could be a better place if more people would lead. Leadership is multifaceted. It is plural, not singular. There are different styles of leadership, but too many approach leadership with a limited definition. When they don't see themselves as influential or well-known, they conclude they are not a leader.

Is leadership style a function of personality or an appropriate choice? Does your leadership style suite your temperament, or does it address a particular situation? I don't believe the answer is an "either/or" but a "both/and." Each person may have a primary leadership style with secondary or supplemental styles. A leader may even have several dominant leadership styles. And each leader needs to know different leadership styles and use them as circumstances dictate. An effective leader will choose his leadership style with a strategic analysis of what is needed in a certain situation.

As we examine varied leadership styles, there are many questions to be answered: What is your dominant style or styles? What would be your secondary or supplemental styles? How well does your leadership style fit your roles where you work or serve? What leadership styles are lacking on your team? What leadership style is needed for a specific opportunity? In order to answer these questions correctly, broad knowledge of leadership styles is necessary.

Daniel Goleman did a landmark study in 2000, published in the *Harvard Business Review* (Goleman 2000), that uncovered six leadership styles. I have given his

styles different names, but his research is helpful in identifying the traits of each style.

Leadership style impacts the organizational culture
more than anything else. How leaders make decisions,
motivate followers, manage change, launch initiatives,
and handle crises is determined by their leadership style.
Leadership styles have a direct impact on the environment and effectiveness of an organization. All of these
styles, when briefly explained, will make sense to anyone
who leads. You'll be able to identify which style fits you
and which styles fit your colleagues.

Visionary

Vision in leadership has been defined as seeing the in-
visible. This is a future-oriented and faith-focused type
of leader. Visionary leaders have a crystal-clear picture
of what they want to happen. They cast vision powerful-
ly. This is usually a senior-level style of leadership. This
leader has great enthusiasm but tends to be somewhat
idealistic. They show how each person's role fits into the
larger vision for the organization. When people work for
this kind of leader, they believe what they do matters. By
framing individual roles within a larger vision, this leader
establishes standards that support the vision. The result
is greater commitment to the organization's goals.

Decisions about opportunities, new initiatives, or other ideas are filtered through the vision. If any of these
things will further the vision, then the leader will champion them. The standard for success is clear to everyone—the implementation of the vision. The visionary
leader understands that vision leaks, it dissipates over

time. A leader with another style might find it repetitive or even irritating to regularly promote the vision, but a visionary leader knows re-casting the vision is a constant responsibility. Finding new ways to describe it or illustrate it are crucial. She constantly looks for stories of how a team member is fulfilling the vision to inspire the other followers.

A visionary will articulate the vision but give followers freedom in how they achieve it. He will allow for experimentation, innovation, and risk-taking. But this leader will always keep the vision focused on the end goals. If this style were summed up in a single phrase, it would be "Come with me." This style works in almost every organizational setting. It is especially effective in an entrepreneurial environment. If you are starting a new business or church where vision is so central to success, this style of leadership is essential. If there is organizational drift or maintenance mentality, and there is clear need for a new vision, the visionary leader can spell out a fresh direction and inspire the people with a powerful vision.

Goleman coined the term "emotional intelligence" (EI) to describe a person's ability to manage themselves and their relationships effectively. Many experts believe EI is as important as IQ in determining personal success—especially leadership effectiveness. EI comprises four fundamental capabilities: self-awareness, self-management, social awareness, and social skill. Each capability contains a certain set of competencies.

There are three specific EI competencies for a person with the visionary leadership style. Self-confidence: a strong and positive sense of self-worth. Empathy: skill at sensing other people's emotions, understanding their perspective, and taking an active interest in their concerns. Change catalyst: proficiency in initiating new ideas and leading people in a new direction. Can you identify with these?

If you are someone who God has given a vision to or someone who can exercise faith, you need to embrace this style. Where changes require a new vision or when clear direction is needed, this style works best. There will always be a place for leaders who inspire an entrepreneurial spirit and create enthusiasm for a new future. This style may not work with a team of experts or those with more experience. The enthusiasm and energy of the leader could become overbearing in certain situations. But more often than not, this style brings great results.

Commander

If the visionary style is the most positive of any leadership style, then the commanding style is the most negative. This leader demands compliance. This style is most effective in a crisis, such as a hostile takeover or to kickstart a company turnaround. This leader makes the tough decisions that need to be made. This style also works well in an actual emergency, like a fire or flood. And it can help with a problem employee when all other approaches have failed.

At a particular critical time, a commanding leader might say, "This is the right path that we should go down." For instance, if a family is at a crossroads and the leader says, "I am going to lead my family down the right path. We are not going to be disloyal or uncommitted. We are not going to be the kind of people who don't honor our word or who don't live according to a set of values. We're not going to take the easy road. We're going to take the path less traveled." God needs a lot more people to exercise that leadership style.

There are three EI competencies of a commanding leader. Achievement orientation: the drive to meet an internal standard of excellence. Initiative: a readiness to seize opportunities. Self-control: the ability to keep disruptive emotions and impulses under control. Do you recognize any of these in your life?

But the impact on the organizational culture with this leadership style is usually very negative. Summed up in a phrase, this style would be "Do what I tell you." Top-down decision-making stifles new ideas. Innovation and flexibility are no longer valued. This style creates fear and leads to bullying. When the leader fires people and then others quit, morale goes to an all-time low. Since bad news is blamed on the messenger, all information stops being communicated.

When people feel alienated, they stop caring about the organization. They no longer act on their own initiative, they lose their sense of ownership, and they function with no accountability. The commanding style takes away pride in achievement, the self-satisfaction of a job well done. It de-motivates people from sharing in the larger mission and feeling like their work makes a difference. Long-term, this style creates an unhealthy culture with a lack of commitment and negative impact.

Harmonizer

The harmonizer style revolves around people. The harmonizing leader values a person's emotions more than tasks and goals. This leader wants to form emotional bonds that create a strong feeling of belonging to the organization. To sum up the style in one phrase, it would be "People come first." The harmonizing leader strives to have unity amongst employees and tries to keep them happy. This style leads to strong communication because people who like each other talk a lot. They share their ideas, they are more open, they trust one another, and this results in greater innovation.

The harmonizing leader will be a good communicator, especially when it comes to sharing her emotions and providing positive feedback. This is very effective in seasons of high stress or when there is some type of trauma. This leader recognizes and rewards work well done. She realizes that much feedback is negative and understands most people receive little encouraging feedback on their work.

This style also allows for greater flexibility. Employees are given freedom to do their job in a way they think is most effective. A harmonizing leader builds a sense of togetherness. She will meet socially with her employees and even individually, taking time to celebrate special occasions like birthdays or team accomplishments. This leader generates great loyalty because of her personal investment, and this style naturally leads to relationship building.

The harmonizing style is effective when trust needs to be repaired, morale needs to be increased, and people need motivation during stressful circumstances. Building team harmony and improving personal communication can bring about a renewed commitment to the mission. The overall energy of the group increases with this leadership. There are three EI competencies of a harmonizing leader. Empathy: skill at sensing other people's emotions, understanding their perspective, and taking an active interest in their concerns. Building bonds: proficiency at cultivating and maintaining a web of relationships. Communication: skill at listening and at sending clear, convincing, and well-tuned messages.

The harmonizing style cannot be used exclusively, because sole reliance on praise and nurturing can foster poor performance. It can lead to a lack of direction, as employees do not receive constructive advice on their performance. Lacking clear directives, the team may in fact be led to failure. This style has a positive impact but needs to be limited to certain situations and defined periods of time.

Producer

This style of leadership gets results. The producing leader sets high standards for performance and expects his employees to model them. He exemplifies these standards himself and is focused on doing things faster and better. This style could be summed up with the phrase "Do as I do—now." He is able to identify poor performers and asks more of them. If they don't improve, he will replace them with people who can.

This style works best when quick results are needed and there is a competent and highly motivated team. If this is lacking, the leader can overwhelm employees with his demands for excellence. The producing leader may know what he wants but not communicate it clearly. He expects people to know what to do. His mantra would be, "If I have to tell you, you're the wrong person for the job." This can lead to employees second-guessing what the leader wants and wondering if the leader trusts them to do their job.

This leader gives little feedback on how people are doing, but if they are not performing, he will take over. This stifles initiative and creates an environment where employees fear doing something wrong. Responsibility dwindles as employees feel little personal investment in their work. Commitment evaporates as people do not see how their personal contribution impacts the larger mission. The overall result can be overwhelmed team members and a lack of innovation.

There are three EI competencies for this style. Conscientiousness: the ability to manage yourself and your responsibilities. Initiative: a readiness to seize opportunities. Achievement orientation: the drive to meet an internal standard of excellence. Can you spot any of these in your own leadership style?

The producing style can work well with certain groups like highly skilled professionals—for example, R&D groups or legal teams. These employees are self-motivated, highly competent, and need little direction. Given a team like this, the producer gets the work done, gets it done excellently, and can even get it done ahead of schedule.

Collaborator

The collaborator style of leadership forges consensus through participation. It is democracy in action—spending time getting people's ideas and, ultimately, their buy-in. The collaborating leader builds a great amount of trust and commitment. By letting employees have direct input into decisions that affect how they do their job, the collaborator increases their ownership. And by listening to their concerns, he learns what is needed for morale to remain strong. The result of this leadership is a fairly realistic understanding of what can and cannot be accomplished in the organization.

The phrase that best sums up this style is "What do you think?" This style is most effective when the leader needs the team to take personal responsibility for a decision, goal, or plan. When the leader is uncertain about the best direction to take, he can receive ideas and input from valuable employees. And if the leader has a clear vision, this style works in generating creative ideas for implementing that vision.

There are two EI competencies for this style. Teamwork and collaboration: competence at promoting cooperation and team building. Communication: skill at listening and at sending clear, convincing, and well-tuned messages. The collaborating leader brings a group of different, diverse people together and builds them into a team that can be much more effective than they could ever be by themselves. If you see these qualities in yourself, this is your leadership style.

One of the real drawbacks to this style is the endless number of meetings where ideas are considered, consensus is not reached, and the result is more meetings. The collaborative leader may actually put off crucial decisions hoping the meetings will yield an unforeseen answer. The outcome can be followers who are confused and directionless. It can even lead to conflicts because of the lack of leadership.

This style does not work well in an emergency situation when time is of the essence and the luxury of endless discussions isn't possible. It also does not work when the team members are not informed enough or competent enough to offer sufficient guidance to the leader. The collaborative leader needs wisdom to know who to listen to and when it is time for a decision to be made.

Coach

The coaching style is focused on developing people. Leaders with this style may at times function more like a counselor who listens to concerns and then guides workers toward a better future path. Coaching leaders help team members identify their strengths and weaknesses. They show how to use them for their personal and professional success and encourage the development of long-term goals and a plan for reaching them. And along the way, they give plenty of input and feedback.

These leaders know how to delegate, not abdicate. They give their team members challenging assignments and opportunities. Some of the tasks will be difficult and may take time to accomplish. They understand that short-term failing can lead to long-term learning. This style is best summed up by the phrase "Try this," and it does not require constant communication to be effective. But the ongoing dialogue ensures people know what is expected of them and how their work fits in the larger vision.

There are three EI competencies for this style. Developing others: the propensity to bolster the abilities of others through feedback and guidance. Empathy: skill at sensing other people's emotions, understanding their perspective, and taking an active interest in their concerns. Self-awareness: the ability to read and understand your emotions as well as recognize their impact on work performance and relationships. If these traits describe you, then you have the coaching style.

This style helps create strong commitment from team members. They respond to the coaching leader's belief and investment in them. When a team member is aware of his weaknesses and wants to improve his performance, this style will be most effective. The style works equally well with team members who understand that coaching will increase the possibility of promotion and advancement.

This style is least effective with team members who are resistant to change or learning new things. It will also not work if the leader does not possess the expertise or proficiency needed to help the person improve. This style requires a somewhat greater degree of time investment than the other styles and may not appear to immediately help the bottom line. But the development of team members will over time yield impressive results for any organization.

. . . . .

Do any of these leadership styles resonate with you? The world, the country, our communities, the church, our families all need more and better leadership. Leaders don't make excuses—they take initiative and get things done. Leaders realize it may be hard, but they do it anyway. It comes down to this: Will you step up to the challenge and lead where God has placed you?

Regardless of your leadership style, there are two principles underlying all effective leadership. First, leaders are servants. Jesus was a servant leader. The Bible tells us Jesus did not come to be served, but to serve (Matthew 20:28). And anyone who leads must have a servant attitude. Leaders use their authority to serve the people, not to boss them around, make them do what they want done, or use the people for their purposes.

Leaders have character. They lead out of a core of integrity and ethics. This is a challenge for leaders, because with authority and power can come corruption. Leaders live by ethical standards. And from a Christian perspective, morality, integrity, and ethics make up the core of what it means to be a leader. Christian leaders live according to a biblical framework. Leaders pursue character, and if they make mistakes, they acknowledge them, learn from them, and then move forward.

God can use you with the leadership style you have. I am convinced things would get better the moment people step up to lead and do what God has led them to do. I've seen the difference leadership can make, and I hope you will use your leadership style to make an impact.

LEADERSHIP STYLES INVENTORY

- For each statement, mark to what extent it is true of your life:

3=VERY

2=SOME

1=LITTLE

0=NOT AT ALL

- Put a number in the blank before each statement.

- Transfer the numbers you gave for each statement to the grid at the end of the inventory.

- Total each column. The highest number identifies your preferred leadership style; the next highest number, your secondary style.

☐ 1. I have a crystal-clear picture of what I want to happen.

☐ 2. I believe in compliance and that it can be effective in a crisis.

☐ 3. I value people's emotions and believe that people come first.

☐ 4. I set high standards for performance and expect others to as well.

☐ 5. I believe consensus is forged through participation.

☐ 6. I like to develop people by listening to their concerns and guiding them toward a better path.

☐ 7. I am very enthusiastic and somewhat idealistic.

☐ 8. I can make the tough decisions that need to be made.

☐ 9. I like to communicate and share ideas.

☐ 10. If you perform poorly I will ask more of you. If you don't improve, I will replace you with someone who can.

☐ 11. My mantra is "What do you think?"

☐ 12. I know how to delegate.

☐ 13. I believe that finding new ways to describe or illustrate the vision is crucial to inspire followers.

☐ 14. I believe in honoring my word and live according to a strict set of values.

☐ 15. I recognize and reward work well done.

☐ 16. I expect people to know what to do. "If I have to tell you, you're the wrong person for the job."

☐ 17. I believe in teamwork and communication.

☐ 18. I My mantra is "Try this."

☐ 19. I allow for experimentation, innovation, and risk-taking while always keeping the vision focused on the end goals.

☐ 20. I don't take the easy road; I favor the path less traveled.

☐ 21. I believe that building team harmony and improving personal communication can bring about a renewed commitment to the mission.

☐ 22. I am conscientious, have initiative, and am achievement oriented.

☐ 23. I need my team to take personal responsibility for a decision, goal, or plan.

☐ 24. I need constant communication with my team to ensure people know what is expected and how their work fits in the larger vision.

1.	2.	3.	4.	5.	6.
7.	8.	9.	10.	11.	12.
13.	14.	15.	16.	17.	18.
19.	20.	21.	22.	23.	24.
Total	Total	Total	Total	Total	Total
Visionary	Commander	Harmonizer	Producer	Collaborator	Coach

CHAPTER NINE

THINKING STYLES

When most of us think about the brain, the terms "left-brained" and "right-brained" come to mind. We have heard before that the human brain is divided into two sections or hemispheres—the left is the logical half while the right is the creative half. The left brain is the center for linguistic expression; it is where logic, language, and analysis originate. The right brain is visual-spatial; it is where creativity, intuition, and imagination come from.

This is the popular understanding of how our brains work, and there are many programs designed to help you use the "other side" of your brain or use both sides more effectively. Left brain/right brain is the predominant way to understand how we think. But neuroscientist Dr. Stephen Kosslyn believes it has no solid basis in science. These sweeping generalizations have actually not stood up to scientific scrutiny. The differences between the right and left sides of the brain are far more nuanced. Overly simplistic dichotomies do not correctly explain how the brain works.

It is tempting to use a simple dichotomy to describe something as complex as the brain. When you examine broad parts of the brain, smaller areas get grouped together. But as the specific region we look at gets larger, the smaller areas being grouped together become more diverse. No single characteristic unites all the small, specialized areas of the brain. The small areas may not have a single function or functions in common. A large region of the brain is more like a rope than a wire, consisting of small overlapping strands rather than a single continuous stand. It is better to think about the brain in terms of systems rather than simple dichotomies.

Kosslyn says the left brain/right brain theory of thinking is actually an urban legend. It sounds right and makes sense, but it is not really true. Where did this myth come from? It all began in 1962 when experimental surgery was done on a very ill epileptic William Jenkins. He was a military veteran who had grand mal seizures—sometimes as many as ten a day.

He learned about Roger Sperry, a renowned neuroscientist at the California Institute of Technology who had been doing experimental work separating the right and left hemispheres of cats and monkeys. Impressed with Sperry's work and desperate for relief from his intractable illness, he agreed to allow Sperry's Caltech team to separate his corpus callosum, which consists of 250 million nerve fibers that connect the two sides of the brain.

Jenkins' surgery went as planned. He recovered without any issues, and his convulsions were gone. Sperry and his team performed follow-up experiments on Jenkins, confirming the theory that each side of the brain has distinct cognitive capabilities. Fifteen more surgeries were done with other epileptics, authenticating the conclusion that the two sides of the brain do in fact have different roles in cognitive functioning. In 1981 Sperry was awarded the Nobel Prize for Medicine/Physiology for his left brain/right brain research.

Articles in *Life Magazine*, *The New York Times Sunday Magazine*, *Psychology Today*, and *Harvard Business Review* all led to greater popularization of the research. A whole new theory of psychology had arisen.

But these new insights were not meant to start a new branch of psychology. In fact, the different capabilities of the right and left brain reflect very specific differences in function. For example, viewing an overall shape versus specific details in perception. Sweeping distinctions such as "logical" versus "intuitive" are far too broad to be accurate.

Researchers have known for decades that these overarching distinctions are not based on solid science. The cultural view of how the brain works is simply not correct. For instance, the left brain is described as verbal and the right brain as perceptual, but both hemispheres play critical roles in extracting meaning out of language. Neuroimaging studies have shown conclusively that many aspects of language processing are appropriated over both hemispheres. Brain imaging has also shown that many aspects of perceptual processing are appropriated over both hemispheres.

Both halves of the brain also play important roles in analytical and creative thinking and in logical and intuitive thought. The popular distinctions actually involve very complex functions accomplished by multiple processes. Some people operate better in the left brain and some better in the right brain, but the functions are not solely in one hemisphere or the other. The two halves work together—they are not isolated or competitive systems.

Why has this incorrect understanding of the brain continued for over fifty years? Why are there YouTube videos like "the Spinning Dancer" testing which side of the brain you use? Why do learning tools promise to help you improve the use of your brain? Why do people like Oprah Winfrey or author Daniel Pink promote this incorrect thinking? The prestige of a Nobel Prize and the power of the Internet are potential answers. And it is also very attractive to explain our thought processes in simplistic ways.

But there is a better way to understand thinking in a simple way. Kosslyn, who for over thirty years was a cognitive neuroscientist and professor of psychology at Harvard University wrote a book with the help of G. Wayne Miller called *Top Brain, Bottom Brain* (Kosslyn and Miller 2013). In it he argues that to understand the functioning of the brain requires a different anatomical division—the bottom and the top part of the brain. He calls this proposal "the Theory of Cognitive Modes." This theory was developed by assembling years of reliable research on the brain mainly known by those in the scientific community.

This research revealed that the top brain uses information about our environment (in concert with other information such as emotional reactions or the need for food or drink) to determine which goals we should attempt to achieve. The top brain formulates a plan and creates expectations about what will happen when the plan is executed. As your plan develops, it compares what is happening with what was expected and adjusts your plan accordingly.

The bottom brain classifies the signals from your senses, comparing the information you perceive with all the information stored in your memory. It then uses the outcomes of the comparisons to classify and interpret the object or event, giving us meaning in life.

Top brain/bottom brain comes from the field of neuropsychology, which is the study of higher cognitive functioning—thoughts, hopes, desires, wishes, and other aspects of your mental life. Higher cognitive functioning is seated in the cerebral cortex, the outer layer of the brain consisting of four lobes. If you view the brain from the side, you can see there is a top and bottom part divided mostly by the Sylvian fissure. The top brain comprises the entire parietal lobe and the larger portion of the frontal lobe. The bottom brain comprises the smaller portion of the frontal lobe and all the occipital and temporal lobes.

The theory provides a new way of understanding how we think and identifies four modes that I refer to as thinking styles. By knowing your thinking style, you can better understand your actions and behaviors and those of others you relate to in various ways. The top and bottom parts of the brain have distinct functions. The top brain devises and executes your plans, like deciding where to move an object or how to move your body. The bottom brain organizes and interprets your incoming information about the world. The parts of the brain always work in concert—the top brain uses information from the bottom brain to formulate and reformulate your plans.

The key is to understand that although the top brain and bottom brain always work together and are both used constantly in your waking hours, you do not rely on them to an equal degree. Except for specific situations (a train coming right at you, for instance) that requires a specific reaction, you can use either system in optional ways. You can use the top brain to create a simple plan or you have the option to use it to create a complex plan.

For example, if you are visiting a new city you can have a simple plan to eat at the nearest restaurant to your hotel. But you could create a more detailed plan to find a highly rated restaurant, coordinate with your friend who lives in that city to meet for dinner, and determine if you will get there by walking, public transportation, or a taxi. You can use your bottom brain to have an immediate sense of what you perceive about the evening or even specific details of the evening. For instance, you can notice the decor of the restaurant, the kind of people who are there, and your friend's appearance.

Each of us is different in how we rely on the two parts of the brain for functioning. Some of us rely on both parts, some rely heavily on the top but not the bottom, some rely heavily on the bottom but not the top and some don't rely heavily on either part. These different four ways your brain may work defines your "cognitive mode." This is your style of thinking about how you approach the world and interact with people. Each person has a unique thinking style that impacts how they relate to people and how they react to situations in their lives.

Before we look at each of the four thinking styles, it is important to clarify a few things. Your thinking style is not related to your intelligence. Intelligence is defined by how easily and quickly you can understand complex material and solve difficult problems. Thinking styles are about how you interact with people and approach situations you encounter. Your distinct thinking style does not determine whether you will have good or bad mental health. It does not make you more or less prone to depression, anger, or worry. And although you have a dominant thinking style, you may adopt another style in a particular context.

But you do have a predominant thinking style you are most comfortable using that guides how you behave and approach life. You did not choose your thinking style—it is most likely the result of your genetic makeup and your experience. How the top brain and bottom brain systems interact produces one of these four thinking styles.

Mover

This thinking style is the result of having both your top and bottom brain systems highly utilized in optional ways. When you think in this style, you implement plans using your top brain, and you register the consequences of doing so using your bottom brain, adjusting your plans based on the feedback you receive. People who have the mover style tend to be leaders. They might lead a church or nonprofit, be an executive in a company, or the president of a school.

If you have this thinking style, you will be very comfortable in positions or situations where you can make a plan, take action, and observe the results of it all. You constantly are looking ahead and considering what plans need to be made. You are a strategic visionary. One-, three-, and five-year plans are simply the way you think. But it is not just planning—it is putting those plans into action that characterizes your life and leadership. And if the plan falters or fails, you will be the first one to think about what went wrong and how you can do it better in the future.

This style has some clear benefits. You are often in a place where you can control your destiny. When you show through your plans and actions how to succeed, people will look to you as a leader and follow your plans. If you do not perform, possibly because of a lack of experience, you can end up offending others and letting them down. Though you likely will accept the feedback and adjust accordingly. This style does require a lot of energy. Envisioning, planning, acting, and altering are all a great amount of work. But if this is your thinking style, you are not typically easily discouraged.

People who have this thinking style include Oprah Winfrey, who overcame a very difficult childhood to build a huge television and publishing empire; President Franklin Roosevelt, who led the US out of the Great Depression and during World War II; and Michael Bloomberg, who created a company that revolutionized how financial information was delivered and went on to twice win election as New York City mayor, even as a Republican.

As I write, I am literally a few miles away from the Wright brothers' monument. Orville and Wilbur Wright endured many failures as they attempted to build the first airplane. They adjusted to the feedback they received, were not easily discouraged, and finally designed the first airplane. I live in Richmond, Virginia, where there is a NASCAR track. Bill France Jr. began by parking cars and working the concession stands at his dad's speedway. And he then expanded car racing from a regional sport into a popular national sport, growing it into a multibillion-dollar business.

Perceiver

In this thinking style, the bottom brain is highly utilized but the top brain is not. When you think like a perceiver, you use your bottom brain system to try and make sense of what you perceive—interpreting your experiences, placing them in a context, and attempting to understand the implications. You may use your top brain to create a narrative that makes sense of what the bottom brain registers, but you do not use your top brain to generate a complex, detailed plan. In other words, the top brain is essentially used in service to the bottom brain.

People who have the perceiver style are usually librarians, novelists, and pastors of smaller churches who generally are not in the limelight. Individuals with this thinking style plays a vital role in groups by providing a big-picture perspective and making sense of events. In the business world they are key members of a team, providing input and wisdom (though not necessarily getting the credit). A perceiver is a good listener and will wait until she has something valuable to share and then will speak up. Because this style results in deeper understanding, she is often worth listening to for counsel.

Perceivers are sensitive observers, advisors, and evaluators. They do not take bold actions or create dramatic results. They also do not seek credit for their input and wisdom. Perceivers are generally in the background occupying the more quiet corners of this world.

This thinking style has distinct advantages. For one, you do not carry the responsibility of leadership and instead have the luxury of stepping back and looking at the big picture. You can take more time to understand a situation. People will recognize your wisdom and seek you out for advice. You can live with less pressure to perform, seek out knowledge for its own sake, and sometimes just live in the moment. You may run into trouble if you do not have enough relevant experience and have little wisdom to offer. You may also spend too much time in reflection and get lost in thought. This may lead you to be too passive and not contribute as much as you should.

A good example of this thinking style is the novelist Emily Dickinson. Dickinson was a conscientious student who briefly attended college but then came home. She had no career ambition and essentially wrote poems and made little effort to publish them. In fact, fewer than a dozen of the 1800 poems she wrote were ever published. Besides caring for her sick mother, her time was her own. She did not create any complex plans or adjust her plans based on environmental feedback. She was a devoted gardener, liked to observe nature, and maybe not surprisingly, wrote poems about the brain. But her poetry is still read to this day, and she is considered to be one of the most significant of all American poets.

Stimulator

This style is when your top brain system is highly utilized but the bottom brain system is not. The stimulator often creates and delivers very detailed plans but then fails to consistently and correctly recognize the consequences of acting on those plans. You don't update or change your plan when events require you to do so. You may be original and creative—able to think outside the box even when others have an established way of approaching a situation. But you may not realize when you have reached a point where your actions are disruptive. And you may not correct your behavior.

You can be a great team player and even provide leadership, but you should not be the only leader to be successful. You operate best when others can help you adjust your plan as circumstances dictate. If this is your thinking style, you may throw out lots of ideas with a certain abandon. Some may be good and stick, others will not. If the good ideas do not succeed, it is because you did not properly fine-tune the plan as you received feedback.

This style does have some clear advantages. For instance, you can create new plans and stick with them, generating some great creative ideas that become reality. Steve Jobs is a perfect example. The impact of his thinking style on Apple, and the subsequent impact of Apple products on our culture, are enormous. If you are good like Jobs was, people may come to you as a source for creative ideas. You certainly have a degree of freedom in not being stressed by small stuff happening around you.

The downside of this style is that you can come on too strong and easily offend others. When you do not alter your plan in response to circumstances, it can create a real problem when it turns out to not be appropriate or helpful to the situation. It can be frustrating for you as well.

You can have a good plan and be blindsided by the results, leaving you feeling unappreciated or misunderstood.

There are many examples of this thinking style in politics with people like former governor Sarah Palin and activist Abbie Hoffman, who both responded poorly when some of their plans went off track. The best example may be Tiger Woods. He clearly uses his top brain and has accomplished as much as anyone ever has in the game of golf. But he does not always respond well to the consequences of carrying out his plans. In his personal life he did not allow his inner circle (caddie, agent, coach) to know what he was doing so they could help him correct his behavior.

Adaptor

Neither the top nor the bottom brain system is highly utilized with the adaptor thinking style. When you have this style, you generally do not initiate plans or focus on interpreting and classifying what you experience. You are simply absorbed by the specific events and immediate conditions of the situation. You are action-oriented and responsive. You tend to "go with the flow" and be seen by others as fun and free-spirited.

Because you can easily embrace the plans of others, you can be a valuable team member. In business you may form the backbone of the company, carrying out essential operations. In the church, adaptors are often volunteers who serve in many vital ministries. You may not formulate a strategy or even contribute much during the planning stage, but once the plan is in place, you will embrace your role and work hard to carry out your assignment.

But if the plan doesn't work out too well, you won't make much of an effort to figure out why and try to fix the problem since you already performed your role.

You will not live in the limelight since you do not devise or carry out complex plans. Nor do you try to understand or interpret circumstances around you. And you can be more easily pushed or pulled by current events. But you do provide an essential infrastructure for an organization, allowing work to get done. You are easy to be with, not stressing about the past and not too worried about the future. You are fun to be around.

Your thinking style has these advantages: When you relax, you can really relax. You are not obsessing over the past or fearful about the future. Because you are easy to get along with and you don't have or push an agenda, people enjoy your company. But you may have some trouble experiencing a lack of control over events in your life. Without a clear direction, you can be buffeted to and fro by the waves of life. (As I write this, there is a storm brewing, and the waves outside my window are crashing into the shore.)

Alex Rodriguez is an example of this thinking style. When he signed with the New York Yankees, he agreed to switch positions from shortstop to third base to accommodate Derek Jeter, showing he was easy to get along with. But he also publically partied and fooled around, ultimately costing him his marriage. And then there was his use of steroids that may cost him his legacy. Elizabeth Taylor is another example. She was a great talent, a rare beauty, and fun to be around. She had fantastic career success, but her personal life was a disaster. She married one wrong man after another, suggesting she had difficulty making the right plans and understanding how her experiences should lead to better choices.

. . . . .

The key to understanding these thinking styles is to recognize how the top brain and the bottom brain systems interact—they should not be seen in isolation. Identifying your style and those of others can help you form successful teams. No one style is better than the other. Each is useful in different circumstances, and each contributes something positive to the team.

THINKING STYLES INVENTORY

- For each statement, mark to what extent it is true of your life:

  3=VERY

  2=SOME

  1=LITTLE

  0=NOT AT ALL

- Put a number in the blank before each statement.

- Transfer the numbers you gave for each statement to the grid at the end of the inventory.

- Total each column. The highest number identifies your preferred thinking style; the next highest number, your secondary style.

☐ 1. I am usually a leader.

☐ 2. I am usually not in the limelight.

☐ 3. I am a great team player.

☐ 4. I tend to "go with the flow."

☐ 5. I am very comfortable making plans, taking action, and observing the results of it all.

☐ 6. I can usually provide a big-picture perspective and make sense of events.

☐ 7. I can create and deliver very detailed plans but can sometimes fail to recognize the consequences of acting on that plan.

☐ 8. Others see me as fun and free-spirited.

☐ 9. I am a strategic visionary constantly planning and putting those plans into action.

☐ 10. I am a good listener and wait until I have something valuable to share and then speak up.

☐ 11. I throw out ideas with abandon. If they don't stick, it is usually because I didn't fine-tune the plan as feedback was received.

☐ 12. I am usually a key player in carrying out essential operations.

☐ 13. I am not easily discouraged.

☐ 14. I don't tend to seek credit for my input or wisdom.

☐ 15. Sometimes I come on too strong and can easily offend others.

☐ 16. I find I can really relax, not obsessing over the past or feeling fearful about the future.

Mover	Perceiver	Stimulator	Adaptor
1.	2.	3.	4.
5.	6.	7.	8.
9.	10	11	12
13.	14.	15.	16.
Total	Total	Total	Total

CHAPTER TEN

FAITH STYLES

All Christ followers need to be a part of the Great Commission Jesus gave when He said, "Go to the people of all nations and make them my disciples" (Matthew 28:19). We all need to do it. But you don't have to do it in a way that isn't natural to you. There are different styles for sharing your faith, and one of these styles will work for you.

In 2 Corinthians 5:18–19 we are told, "God has done it all! He sent Christ to make peace between himself and us, and he has given us the work of making peace between himself and others. What we mean is that God was in Christ, offering peace and forgiveness to the people of this world. And He has given us the work of sharing His message about peace."

Jesus has given us the work of sharing his message. We are to share our faith. It's not enough for you to know Christ—the gospel needs to be shared with other people.

It is important we all understand what the gospel is, whether you are a seeker, a new follower of Christ, or a maturing follower of Christ. The gospel literally means "the good news." The good news is that God has done it all. We don't have to do anything. You don't earn your way into heaven. You can't do enough good works. It is not a matter of you doing more good things than bad things so you end up in heaven. God has done it all. He sent Christ to make peace between himself and us. But why do we need peace? God is perfect; we are not. That is the problem. We are sinful, and thus there is enmity between humanity and God.

Jesus solved the problem by offering forgiveness to the people of this world. He came to earth, lived a sinless life, died on the cross for all the sins of humanity, and then rose from the grave, proving His victory over sin and death. Now, when we accept Jesus, we are forgiven of all our sins. God doesn't see our imperfections—he sees Jesus in us. And we're now at peace with God. That is the gospel in a nutshell.

The gospel message needs to be shared. Everyone on this earth needs to know they can have a spiritual life. They can be born spiritually. Having a spiritual life and connecting with God makes your life completely different. You can entirely miss what life is really all about. It's not just about the physical or the material. It's about the spiritual. And it isn't just a certain kind of person who shares their faith. Everyone can do it once you identify your faith style.

A lot of people have misunderstandings about sharing the gospel. Because they have misunderstandings, they don't want to do it. Let's clear up all the misunderstandings and show you how God has given you a natural way to share your faith. You can share in a style that is true to who you are. People desperately need to hear the Good

News. People need an accurate understanding of God. Too many people have misunderstandings about God. People hear things when they are growing up that cause them to form the impression that God is angry. God is grumpy. God is mean. God is not any of those things. God is love. All love begins with God. The central message of Christianity is to love God and love others.

How do we clear up all these misunderstandings? We need to share the truth. God has given us the work of sharing His message about peace between God and humanity. There are different approaches that you can take. There isn't a one-size-fits-all approach. There is a style that suits each individual. And one of these styles suits you. These styles come from the book *Becoming a Contagious Christian* by Mark Mittelberg and Bill Hybels (Hybels and Mittelberg 1994). As you read about these styles, you can identify the one that's most natural for you.

We can't leave it up to other people to share the gospel. No one person or one group of people can possibly reach everyone. All of us need to share the message. We simply need to identify what style is most natural for us, what approach we can take that we're most comfortable with.

Testimonial Style

The testimonial style simply involves telling your story of faith. It doesn't have to be a dramatic story, but it can be. Recently I heard a man share his incredible story. He started drinking whiskey at nine years old. Then he graduated up to alcohol and drugs. His life was a complete and total mess. He shared his story of finding peace through accepting Christ. It was dramatic, no doubt about it, but you don't need that kind of testimony to share your story. Some people won't relate to a dramatic story. What is your story? Whatever it is, you share your story because people need to be able to relate. And they might relate to your story better than the more dramatic story.

In the Bible this style is illustrated by the story of a blind man in John 9. He was blind and Jesus healed him. And when he was healed of his blindness, he got pretty excited and began to tell everybody what happened to him. His testimony was simply, "I was blind and now I see." The testimonial style is where you tell your story. "This is the person I was. This is how I came to know Christ and receive the gospel message into my life. And this is the way I am now." For some, this feels very natural to share.

The reason it feels natural has to do with the qualities you have in your life. Someone with a testimonial style is a good listener, and they like to listen to other people. Someone who has this testimonial style is able to tell their story naturally and comfortably while keeping the gospel at the center of it. First John 1:3 says, "We are telling you what we have seen and heard, so that you may share in this life with us. And we share in it with the Father and with his Son Jesus Christ." You're telling what you've seen and heard. We're just telling your story. If you can do that and feel comfortable, then this testimonial style is for you.

This style can be very significant in our culture with famous people. Someone like Tim Tebow has an incredible story. His mother was told she should have an abortion, and she chose not to do it. Tim was born and becomes this fantastic star football player. And he now has an opportunity to share his story with other people. There is a man who lost over two hundred pounds on *The Biggest Loser,* and now he's now sharing his story of faith. Russell Wilson is from Richmond, Virginia, where I live, and he played at the same time as my youngest son Wes. Wilson has a marvelous testimony. As the Super Bowl-winning quarterback of the Seattle Seahawks, he has a platform to share his testimony. When famous people share their story, it can have a powerful impact—and so can you.

Interpersonal Style

Relationships are built over time with the interpersonal style, and you simply share the gospel within the context of your relationship. The relationship already exists. You don't just walk up to a stranger and say, "Hey, do you know about Jesus?" That generally does not work. What does work is relationship. In the Bible we see this style with Jesus's disciple Matthew, who wrote the first book of the New Testament. Matthew was a tax collector; he was a businessman and had a lot of business contacts. When he became a follower of Jesus, he knew a lot of people that he could talk to about Jesus.

Someone who is interpersonal is a people person—the kind of person that loves to be around people and gets energy from being around others. Interpersonal individuals are talkers, who like conversation and can carry a conversation. So the interpersonal style suits those who are really focused on relationships and think relationships are valuable, important, and significant. First Corinthians 9:22 says: "When I am with people whose faith is weak, I live as they do to win them. I do everything I can to win everyone I possibly can." If this is your faith style, this means that when you are around people who don't know Christ, you are not judging them. You are just hanging out with them. You are relating to them. You don't think you shouldn't be friends with them because they are not a follower of Christ. You are a good friend. And out of that relationship, you are able to share the gospel at the appropriate time.

Your friend may notice how you seem to always be joyful even though you have problems like they do. You just seem to handle your problems better. Or they may notice you just seem to have good things happen to you. They may wonder why you seem to be so blessed. They may even ask themselves about how you live under the blessings of God. If they ask you something like that, be honest and tell them about your relationship with Christ.

Interpersonal individuals like to have people over to their house. They like to entertain. They like to meet for coffee or lunch. These are the people who like to go to social events, meet new people, and make new friends. However, you will have to practice patience and wait for spiritual opportunities. You may know someone for three months and never get a chance to share with him at all. Maybe months go by and then one day he wants to do something or go somewhere on a Sunday. You could say, "Well, I can do something on Saturday, but I have be back to go to church on Sunday." He may then say, "You go to church?" What do you like about going?" And now you have an opportunity to share the gospel.

You are not preaching—you just share. You tell them your experience. You do have to be careful because you can get overwhelmed with the numerous needs of your friends. One friend might be struggling financially, another friend's marriage might be in trouble, still another friend might have a health problem, and a fourth may have just lost his job. This can be overwhelming, so you have to be wise, but it is very important to let God use you in the right situation.

Direct Style

The direct style is bold and to the point. You just tell people the way it is. The apostle Peter had this style. He stood up in front of thousands of people in Acts 2. He essentially said to all these people, "This is the deal. This is who Jesus is. The one that you crucified is the Messiah and the Savior of the world. And you need to come to him and receive forgiveness!" And 3,000 people came to Christ right there.

This kind of person is direct, but they get results. People respond to it. A person with this style will clarify truth and challenge people to accept Christ. They will tell people they are not perfect and God is. They will tell people doing more good things than bad will not get you into heaven. They will challenge people to accept the forgiveness that God offers through Jesus Christ. They lay it out there with not a lot of fluff or even sensitivity.

Second Timothy 4:2 says, "Preach God's message. Do it willingly, even if it isn't the popular thing to do. You must correct people and point out their sins, but also cheer them up . . . when you instruct them." So the Bible tells us to point out where things need to change. But you also need to be encouraging. You can inspire and motivate while also pointing out sin and calling people to change.

The direct individual has strong convictions. They are not necessarily someone who deals in a lot of small talk. They want to talk about the macro, the big picture. The interpersonal style person can talk about the micro, smaller things. They prefer the bigger, larger issues to be addressed immediately. This person has to exercise a lot of wisdom and recognize there is a time to speak and there is a time to not speak. This person needs to be an active listener. They are usually more inclined to want to talk, but they sometimes need to listen first. They need to value what people have to say. Rather than preach at people, they have to value their story, their journey, how they got to where they are. They have to find out some things like bad experiences or other situations that have negatively impacted the way they think about God or Christianity.

A person with this style needs to be tempered. Truth and love will always need to be held in balance. The Bible tells us to "speak the truth in love" (Ephesians 4:15). Speak the truth, but speak it in love. Don't shove the gospel down people's throats if you have the direct style. This can be done, and Billy Graham is the most prominent example.

Intellectual Style

The intellectual style uses ideas, evidence, and logic. Individuals with this style want to spell out the evidence for faith. I had dinner with a friend of mine who is this kind of person. He is working on his fourth college degree.

I earned my three degrees before I was thirty—he is almost fifty and still wanting to learn more. We were talking about what he is studying and all these things that he's doing. He loves to debate and discuss Christianity. He wants to ultimately do it full-time for a living.

In the Bible, the apostle Paul was this kind of person. He was highly educated, as educated as anyone in ancient times. He studied under the number one rabbi of his day. Paul was a serious student. This is part of the reason why he wrote almost half of the New Testament—because he had a great degree of education. He was someone who liked to debate and discuss Christianity. In Acts 17 we see Paul goes to Athens to a place called Mars Hill where all the philosophers hung out. He went there to discuss and debate the philosophers of his day. He discussed and debated with these philosophers about who Jesus was. Later Paul went to the Forum in Rome and discussed Jesus. I walked among the ruins of the ancient Forum in Rome recently. It was a place designed for intellectual discourse and open debate of ideas. Paul loved to be in such a setting and share the gospel.

Intellectuals are comfortable with discussion, a free flow of ideas, and the challenge to make their case. If this is your style, it is important to know you can be analytical without being argumentative. And it's tricky to avoid turning everything into an argument. Remember that you can show analytically that the things you believe are true. You don't want to be a person who is known for arguing more than for what you actually believe.

I Peter 3:15 says, "Always be ready to give an answer when someone asks you about your hope." Those with an intellectual style always has an answer. They can answer the big questions like, "What about evil?" What about suffering in this world? Why do bad things happen?" They are comfortable with the tough questions because they have spent a lot of time considering them. But attitude is as important as information for this intellectual style. If your attitude is bad, your information can never be received. So the attitude has to be right and people can then receive the information.

Some key people with this style are William Craig Lane, probably the premiere debater in the world today for Christianity. He's an academic. He's an intellectual. He does not get drawn into acting argumentative or negative. He simply presents the case for faith in Christ. Ravi Zacharias is another person with this style. He speaks at many college campuses. He makes outstanding intellectual arguments for the gospel using a wide range of history, philosophy, science, art, and Scripture. The former journalist Lee Strobel is another person with this style. He explains Christianity in very easy to understand terms. If this is your style, embrace your intellect.

Serving Style

People with a serving style help others, and in doing so, they illustrate God's love. They serve first through actions, which later leads to serving with words. In the Bible, there is a woman named Dorcas (also known as Tabitha). In Acts 9:36 it says that Dorcas, or Tabitha, made clothes for the widows and the poor, and she did it to show God's love. Though clothes are still expensive in our modern day, they were even more so in biblical times. There were no stores to purchase clothes—no Nordstrom, no Macy's.

So someone making clothes and giving those clothes away was a big deal.

Individuals with a serving style tend to be more shy, more introverted, and more reserved. There are some who believe they cannot share the gospel, even though we are all commissioned to do so. They think they are not the type of person who can share their faith. If you are that person, maybe you can share your faith through the good works that you do. Matthew 5:16 tells us, "Make your light shine so that others see the good that you do and will praise your Father in heaven." Go serve at the food pantry, go feed the homeless, go read to the at-risk children in your city. When you do, you are showing God's love in a practical way, and people see it.

A person who has this style sees value in any task that's done for God. They'll do anything. They'll wash something, scrub something, take something, make something. They see it as showing the gospel message of God's love.

If you're a serving person, your actions need to be balanced with words. It can't always just be doing things and never saying anything about why you do what you do. It's not about being a good guy or a nice lady. It's not about people liking you or thinking you are special. It's about whom you represent. You have to communicate the spiritual motivation behind your acts of service. "Why am I doing this? Because I want to do good works that bless people and show God's love in practical ways." That is the motivation.

Invitational Style

If you have an invitational style, you are an inviter. You ask a friend, coworker, or relative to come to a church service you know will be helpful to them in some way. You invite them to a concert with contemporary Christian music. You invite them to hear a well-known person or celebrity share their testimony. You may invite them to a conference that has a specific theme or is geared toward men or women. You are intentionally looking for opportunities to invite.

In John 4 there is a powerful picture of this style. There is a Samaritan woman who is not supposed to be addressed by a Jewish man. Jesus talks to her anyway and tells her things about herself that no one could possibly know. She is so impacted by her experience with Jesus that she goes back to her village and tells everyone they need to meet and listen to this man. Next they invited Jesus back to their village. Jesus spent two entire days in that village sharing his message. And the Bible says in verse 42, "And many came to believe." This Samaritan woman simply invited her fellow villagers to hear the message.

Maybe you are this kind of person. You like to meet people—the more people, the better. You are passionate about the gospel and firmly believe that if more people could hear the Good News, more people's lives would be positively changed. My wife has this style. She may come with me on a trip, and she loves when we meet new people. She has invited an amazing number of people to attend our church over the years.

People with this style are persuasive. They are in many ways salespeople for Jesus. And I mean that in the most positive way. They believe there is no greater message than the gospel, and they want everyone to hear it. They're persistent and do not get discouraged by hearing the word *no*. They just keep on inviting. If they see an opportunity, they are motivated and have hope. They are ready to invite and help people experience a relationship with God.

Luke 14:23 is says, "Go out along the back roads and fence rows and make people come in, so that my house will be full." Jesus tells a story about a banquet to illustrate God's desire that his house would be full. He wants everyone to have the chance to hear the gospel. And when people invite, they have that opportunity. People who have this style have the ability to get people to come with them. And if you've got this style, you can encourage people to come with you and connect with God.

· · · · ·

We all need to be a part of this marvelous commission. We need to share the gospel. It is a work we've been given to do. But you don't have to do it in a way that isn't natural to you. You were created a certain way, and you need to function within that style. One of these six styles works for you, and you need to identify which one it is and use it for Christ.

FAITH STYLES INVENTORY

- For each statement, mark to what extent it is true of your life:

  3=VERY

  2=SOME

  1=LITTLE

  0=NOT AT ALL

- Put a number in the blank before each statement.

- Transfer the numbers you gave for each statement to the grid at the end of the inventory.

- Total each column. The highest number identifies your preferred faith style; the next highest number, your secondary style.

1. I often mention my personal background or experience in order to illustrate a point I am trying to make.

2. I am a "people person" who places a high value on friendship.

3. In conversations, I like to approach topics directly, without much small talk or "beating around the bush."

[ ] 4. I have a hard time getting out of a bookstore without buying a bunch of new books that will help me understand what people are thinking.

[ ] 5. I see needs in people's lives that others often overlook.

[ ] 6. I enjoy adding or including new people in activities I'm involved in.

[ ] 7. I often identify with others by using phrases like, "I used to think that, too," or "I once felt the way you do."

[ ] 8. People have commented about my ability to develop deep friendships.

[ ] 9. I don't shy away from challenging someone when it seems necessary.

[ ] 10. I tend to be analytical and logical.

[ ] 11. I find fulfillment in helping others, often in behind-the-scenes ways.

[ ] 12. To be honest, I often watch for situations in which someone "better qualified" can explain concepts to my friends.

[ ] 13. When I talk around the locker room or drinking fountain, people really listen.

☐ 14. I would rather delve into personal life issues than abstract theoretical ideas.

☐ 15. I do not have a problem confronting my friends with the truth even if it strains the relationship.

☐ 16. In conversations, I naturally key in on questions that are holding up a person's understanding or progress.

☐ 17. I would rather show love through actions than through words.

☐ 18. It is not unusual for me to attend special events or concerts and bring along a car full of friends.

☐ 19. I intentionally share my mistakes and struggles with others when it will help them consider solutions that could help them.

☐ 20. I prefer discussions about a person's life before getting into the details of their beliefs and opinions.

☐ 21. I think the world would be a lot better place if people would stop being so sensitive about everything and just speak the truth!

☐ 22. I enjoy discussions and debates on difficult questions.

[ ] 23. I have found that my quiet demonstrations of love and care sometimes help people open up and become more receptive to what I think.

[ ] 24. I tend to watch for worthwhile events to bring people to (such as enriching seminars, retreats, classes or church services).

[ ] 25. People seem interested in hearing stories about things that have happened in my life.

[ ] 26. I enjoy long talks with friends and it doesn't matter much where we are or where we're going.

[ ] 27. A motto that would fit me is: "Make a difference or a mess, but *do* something."

[ ] 28. Often when listening to teachers or TV commentators, I mentally (or even verbally) argue with their positions and logic.

[ ] 29. I think the world would be a better place if people would talk less and take more action on behalf of their friends and neighbors.

[ ] 30. I am always looking for a match between the needs and interests of my friends and various books, classes, and programs that they would enjoy or benefit from.

[ ] 31. I am still amazed at how God has worked in my life, and I would like others to know about it.

☐ 32. People generally consider me to be an interactive, sensitive, and caring kind of person.

☐ 33. I sometimes get in trouble for lacking gentleness and sensitivity in the way I interact with others.

☐ 34. I like to get at the deeper reasons for opinions that people hold.

☐ 35. I tend to be more practical and action-oriented than philosophical and idea-oriented.

☐ 36. A highlight of my week is when I can take a guest with me to a helpful learning event, including church.

1.	2.	3.	4.	5.	6.
7.	8.	9.	10.	11.	12.
13.	14.	15.	16.	17.	18.
19.	20.	21.	22.	23.	24.
25.	26.	27.	28.	29.	30.
31.	32.	33.	34.	35.	36.
Total	Total	Total	Total	Total	Total
Testimonial	Interpersonal	Direct	Intellectual	Serving	Invitational

CHAPTER ELEVEN

GIVING STYLES

G iving gifts is a part of life. There are Christmas gifts, birthday gifts, anniversary gifts, wedding gifts, baby gifts, and the list goes on. There are stores that try to generate business by creating registries where people can identify the gifts they want others to buy for them. They will even assign a special salesperson to assist with the registry process. Of course if a registry isn't available, finding the right gift becomes our responsibility. Hardly anyone gets out of buying gifts for other people. It is such a customary part of life that you may have never thought about how you do it.

The *Journal of Consumer Research* reported on a study conducted at the University of Illinois in which researchers went with people Christmas shopping to discover their gift giving strategies (Belk 1976). They accompanied a number of people over several days as they went shopping for Christmas gifts, observing and noting their pattern of purchasing different gifts. Out of their research, they identified six strategies for gift buying what I will refer to as six giving styles. What makes these styles unique from some other styles is how someone may use a different giving style depending on the relationship they have with their recipient. So a person might purchase gifts for their spouse one way but another way for their coworker or in-laws. I think these giving styles are interesting, enlightening, and common to all. These styles are used differently at one time or another by at least some of us if not all of us.

Pleaser

In the University of Illinois study, the pleaser was the most common style for gift buying. Pleasers want to get the perfect gift. They listen whenever people talk about things they like, and then they go out and purchase that gift they know the person is going to enjoy so much. Individuals with this style, at least some of the time, are often really hoping for an acknowledgment of how perfect the gift was. They want praise—affirmation that the gift was exactly what the person wanted. A person with this style of giving is seen as thoughtful and appreciates that acknowledgment.

Provider

The provider is a person who buys gifts that people need. This is the husband who buys his wife a blender. Some would ridicule the man because he might say, "You said you wanted a blender. You said you could make smoothies and you would lose weight if you had a blender. I got you a blender for your birthday." These are the kind of people who buy tools for guys who want tools and software for the girl who needs it for her computer. They buy practical things for people that are in need. If a family member needs a new dishwasher, they buy that for them, whether it is Christmas or their anniversary. At Christmas they might buy necessities for needy children that are distributed through their church, like a new coat or a pair of sneakers. Providers often purchase gifts that someone wouldn't necessarily get for themselves.

Socializer

The socializer is the kind of person who buys gifts for people that they want them to have. They say, "You would look great in this kind of outfit, so I'm going to buy it for you and you'll just look fantastic. You wouldn't buy it for yourself because you don't have enough fashion sense. But fortunately, I do! I'm going to help you look better than you've looked before." This is the kind of person who buys gifts that are self-help oriented—books, CDs, and DVDs that will encourage and inspire people. But the intent of this particular type of giver is to communicate that their gifts can help you in some way. This is also the giving style that most involves gift cards. The amount of people buying gift cards has risen significantly. A socializer buys gift cards and gives them to whomever so they can buy whatever they want. They are not uncomfortable with it, even if the dollar amount is displayed or they are not personal enough.

Compensator

The compensator is the kind of person who tries to make up for something with their gift giving. Many who have this style use the Christmas gift-giving season as *the* way to do that. Parents who have divorced will try to compensate for how bad they feel about the impact on their children, so they'll make up for it with some kind of big gift or series of gifts. Compensators will also use this season of the year as a way to make up for a lack of loving words or actions throughout the year. This is the person who buys something they really want and then wrap it for themselves and put it under the tree. I might know something about this, especially at Christmas. Many times while shopping for others I will find something I want at a price I like. Then I give it to my wife to gift back to me. This system works out well since I'm not be the easiest person to buy for.

Acknowledger

Acknowledgers give out of a sense of duty—usually small gifts, though not always. This kind of gift giving happens when a person receives a gift and then feels obligated to give a gift in return. It can be like the second round of Christmas cards folks send out. They send out a first round of cards, then they get cards from individuals they didn't send a card to, so they send out more cards in return. It is a reciprocal type of giving. Interestingly, the University of Illinois researchers discovered that regifting is most common among acknowledgers—the practice of taking a gift you received that you really didn't want, never opened, never used, never wore, and simply recycling it. It is gift giving, if not a little unusual for some.

Avoider

I'm sure the researchers had the most fun observing avoiders. This style of giver is the Scrooge of Christmas. They really don't want to give gifts, go through the effort of purchasing gifts, or try to find out what people want. So they give as little as they can. Their thinking is that they can't give to everyone, so only a few people will get gifts. It is a begrudging way of giving that they rationalize or justify it in their own mind. At Christmas they say it has become commercialized so they don't want to buy into the commercialization. For other gift-giving occasions they think that people already have enough junk, and don't want to contribute to their junk pile with more stuff they don't need. This giving style is really a nongiving style. The avoider does not want to give gifts and does not see gift giving as valuable or important.

. . . . .

What is most interesting about these giving styles as opposed to other styles we have talked about in this book is how they depend on individuals' relationships. A person's giving style can actually be dependent on their recipient. I think that is very insightful and very fascinating.

These giving styles originate out of our need or obligation to give gifts. Gift giving dates back thousands of years, but God changed the entire nature of giving when he gave us Jesus. Romans 8:32 tells us, "God did not keep back his own Son, but gave him for us." This is a powerful and significant Scripture in the Bible. In fact, Romans 8 is an important chapter in the Bible that is key in understanding Christianity because it contains the basic beliefs and message. Even if you are already a follower of Christ, if you want to establish a better understanding of what Christianity is all about, Romans 8 is a good chapter to read.

The Greatest Giver

Of the several very well-known and significant verses in Romans 8 is verse 32. This is a linkage verse with another very famous scripture in the Bible—John 3:16: "For God so loved the world he gave his only Son, that whoever believes in him shall not perish but have eternal life" (NIV). God did not keep back his Son, but he gave him for us. So the whole concept, the whole foundation of gift giving finds its root and foundation in our understanding of who God is. God is the greatest giver. He is the original giver. He is the best giver. And the very best gift he could have possibly given was his gift of Jesus. God knew there was a problem with human sinfulness and his perfection. How do you span that enormous chasm? How does a perfect God have a relationship with imperfect people?

How does a God who is holy have a relationship with people whose sins, transgressions, shortcomings, weaknesses, and failures keep them far from him? God's plan was Jesus. He would be the one mediator between God and humanity. God gave us Jesus. Jesus was a gift that was planned. The Bible tells us from the beginning that God knew the plan. The Old Testament prophets prophesied that someday there would be a Messiah. There would be a Savior of the world. In ancient times, people's relationship with God involved sacrifices and living by a very strict law that they could never live up to. The prophets foresaw that in the future God would make a new covenant based on grace, and Jesus would be the foundation. He is the perfect gift because he meets the need that no one else can meet. He saves us. What are we saved from? We are saved from our imperfection. We are saved from the fact that we're not acceptable to God. We are saved from eternal separation from God. And because of Jesus, we're forgiven. His work on the cross gives us the opportunity to receive forgiveness. It doesn't mean we are forgiven automatically. We must ask to be forgiven. However, anyone that asks to be forgiven will be forgiven. They will receive forgiveness, and then they will have a relationship with God through Jesus.

But God's plan involved sacrifice, as all giving does. However you want to look at it, whatever way you want to see it, giving always involves sacrifice. In order to give something, you have to give up something, whether it's something small or something big. God's sacrifice was big—it was the greatest sacrifice. And He was willing to give us Jesus because there was no other way for the problem of human sin to be solved.

God continues to give. The rest of Romans 8:32 says, "If God did this, won't he freely give us everything else?" God's giving doesn't end with the gift of Jesus. Rather, it continues and expands with Jesus. There can be no single greater gift than Jesus, no greater quality gift than Jesus, but the quantity of gifts can be far greater, because over and over again God chooses to bless us. God chooses to consistently and freely give to us. What we receive in our lives is grace, gifts, and blessings.

We receive from God consistently and continually throughout our lives. What should our response be to God's generous giving? Those who have accepted the gift of Jesus, who say they are followers of Christ, should give like God gives. We will be givers because God is the greatest giver. There is no greater way to follow Christ than to be a generous and giving person. Nothing a person can do marks their Christ followership better than the way in which they are generous giver. It is interesting how this seminal, significant indicator that someone understands the giving nature of God—responding with a giving nature towards others—can be an issue for so many. My many years of pastoral experience have shown me that people can follow Christ in other kinds of ways, but they find it very difficult to be a generous, giving person. It is strange and somewhat illogical that the first thing that should be done is not done. The most significant and basic way to follow Christ and to have a relationship with him would be to connect with God's basic giving nature, yet it is a challenge for people.

There are so many opportunities to show our giving heart. Gift giving is greater than just holidays and special occasions. There are three kinds of giving taught in the Bible. There are gifts to the poor, which is called alms. The second way to give is offerings. These are gifts given for special needs or occasions like missions, building projects, disaster relief, and more. The third way to give is tithing—the tenth of our income that we give to the church regularly throughout the year. These three kinds of giving are different types of gifts that God wants us to give.

It is a sacrifice to give. To give means there are going to be resources that are no longer at your disposal, but the model of sacrifice has been given to us. How can we not follow, if we are true followers of Christ? If we are Christians not just in name only but in actual practice, then sacrificial giving is a part of what we do. It is a part of who we are. It is not an occasional thing—it has got to be consistent. There may be one time a year that we buy some gifts for children in need, maybe during Christmas, but there will always be opportunities to give. Giving doesn't just have seasonal elements to it. It is something we do all the time. It is something we do willingly, just as God was willing to give. The Bible says God loves a cheerful giver (2 Corinthians 9:7). Before it says that we should be cheerful givers too, it tells us not to give under compulsion or because we feel forced to give. God doesn't want us to behave like an avoider who only gives because they feel they have to. That is not the kind of giver that God wants to see in us. He wants to see a person who is cheerful and happy about the opportunity to give. A generous person with a giving heart doesn't evaluate their giving by how good it makes them feel. They give because it is the right thing to do.

Giving is right to do all the time—it can't just be for a birthday, an anniversary, or Christmas. As followers of Christ, we are consistent givers. We don't wait until just certain times of the year to do it. We are always looking for opportunities to follow Jesus's example. We know what Jesus would do. God's heart is generosity. God's heart is giving. It is so important to give—to give freely, to give sacrificially, to give consistently, and most of all, to give generously.

GIVING STYLES INVENTORY

- For each statement, mark to what extent it is true of your life:

3=VERY

2=SOME

1=LITTLE

0=NOT AT ALL

- Put a number in the blank before each statement.

- Transfer the numbers you gave for each statement to the grid at the end of the inventory.

- Total each column. The highest number identifies your preferred giving style; the next highest number, your secondary style.

1. I listen to what people like so that I can give the perfect gift.

2. I like to give gifts that people need.

3. I like to buy gifts for people that I want them to have.

☐ 4. I like to give gifts during the holidays to make up for something bad that has happened.

☐ 5. Sometimes I give out of a sense of duty, even though the gift may be small.

☐ 6. I find gift-giving to be too much effort because I don't want to try to find out what the person really wants.

☐ 7. I want affirmation from the person receiving the gift that it was exactly what they wanted.

☐ 8. I like to give gifts to people that they would not buy for themselves.

☐ 9. I think great gifts are self-help books to encourage and inspire people.

☐ 10. Sometimes I give to a person during the holidays to make up for our bad relationship during the year.

☐ 11. If I receive a gift, then I need to give a gift in return.

☐ 12. Holidays have become too commercial, and I don't want to buy into that.

☐ 13. People see me as a thoughtful giver.

☐ 14. When I give on holidays, it is usually a needed gift, not necessarily a wanted gift.

15. I love to give gift cards.

16. I may have bought a gift for myself, wrapped it up, and put it under the Christmas tree.

17. I have been known to regift.

18. I think that people have enough junk, so I don't want to add to it with more stuff they don't need.

1.	2.	3.	4.	5.	6.
7.	8.	9.	10.	11.	12.
13.	14.	15.	16.	17.	18.
Total	Total	Total	Total	Total	Total
Pleaser	Provider	Socializer	Compensator	Acknowledger	Avoider

CHAPTER TWELVE

RETIREMENT STYLES

W hat comes to mind when you hear the word *retirement*? Some may still think of traditional retirement—working until you are sixty-five and then relying on the money you have saved and social security for income. Planning for retirement is solely focused on money. And the retirement years are essentially lived as an extended vacation.

But there are powerful questions that need to be asked, such as "Who do I want to be? What is it that can make me a better person? What have I missed? What am I wired for? What makes me feel most alive, connected, and happy?"

There is a new way of viewing retirement and planning for it. With this change comes both new opportunities and new responsibilities. People are retiring at a younger age. When I attended a retirement seminar, I was surprised at how early many people in the room were planning to retire. The average age was close to sixty. Interestingly, my neighbors both just retired at sixty.

We are living longer than previous generations and in better health. Only a few thousand people lived to be 100+ in 1950, but by 2010, the number had grown to over 300,000 people with the highest numbers in the US and Japan. The amount of time we spend in retirement could span one third of our entire life. And many want an active, independent lifestyle that has purpose. They view retirement as a new, exciting chapter of life.

Baby boomers constitute about 30 percent of our population. The Pew Research Center reported (Heimlich 2010) that beginning in 2011 and continuing to 2030, 10,000 baby boomers a day will turn sixty-five. What will all these people do in retirement? Boomers want to look and act young. They want to stay connected and creative. And according to the MetLife Mature Marketing Institute, 91 percent of pre-retirees (age fifty to sixty-five) want to live in their homes after retirement.

But these individuals are not a homogenous group. There are in fact different retirement styles. These styles reflect a variety of approaches to retirement. Some want a future dedicated to relaxation. Others want learning and engagement. Still more want adventure or contribution. Boomers are more likely to move toward a fuller life rather than gearing down in retirement. They see themselves as vibrant and energetic, and though they may want to retire from their job, they do not want to retire from life.

The first thirty years of life is the Becoming Stage, where we prepare both personally and professionally. This is the time of becoming an adult, earning degrees and certifications, and developing skills. All of this builds a foundation for us to achieve success in a career, feel engaged, and experience a level of satisfaction. The next thirty years is the Being Stage, where we get married, raise a family, and pursue a career. The career may be one we are passionate about, just a source of steady employment, or entail moving from one job to another. The final years are the Redefining Stage. This may be the time of greatest control over our lives. Who we are, what we want to do, and where we want to go.

In the Becoming Stage we are too young, immature, and controlled by outside forces to determine our destiny. In the Being Stage, life demands we focus on family and career. Now in the Redefining Stage we can finally take the knowledge, skills, and experience we have acquired and determine what to do next. We now have time, marketable skills, health, financial security, and numerous relationships to inform our redefining direction.

Retirement happens. Whether you have already retired or your retirement looms ahead in the future, clearly identifying your retirement style will make your retirement so much more fulfilling. Defining how you want to live the last third of your life is essential. In Carolee Duckworth and Marie Langworthy's book *Shifting Gears to Your Life & Work After Retirement*, they spell out seven retirement pathways that I will call retirement styles (Duckworth and Langworthy 2013). Three of the styles are more classical or traditional and four are more modern or contemporary.

Unlike some styles that are hardwired in us, you can choose your retirement style. Retirement is a new time when anything is possible. You may have cut quite a groove (or rut) in your pre-retirement life, but now you can break free from the past and fashion a new you. It is exciting to think of what the rest of your life may look like as you consider what style is right for you.

Leisure

This may be the most traditional retirement style. The leisure style still appeals to many boomers and often involves moving to Florida or Arizona, buying a house near a golf course, and enjoying rest and relaxation. Leisure activities are the priority, and daily life is centered on them. Hobbies that were pursued in the past now can be focused on in earnest. Hobbies that were never pursued because of other time commitments can finally be taken up.

Certain people may find this style very attractive. The CEO who has worked eighty hours a week for years, traveled constantly, and loved his vacations but never had enough of them might choose this style. The small business owner who worked six days a week for years, hardly ever took a vacation, and lived with the stress of meeting payroll each week could be attracted to this style.

It would not be strange for anyone with a high-powered, high-stress, high-profile job to leave their demanding profession and pursue a much more leisurely life. They might not want to have lunch with former colleagues or be invited to others retirement parties—they simply want to fade off into the sunset never to be heard from again.

Is leisure your retirement style? Is there a sport you enjoy like golf or fishing? Is there a hobby you love but never had the time to pursue? Is there a skill you always wanted to develop more fully? Could you find contentment in spending your days in these kinds of pursuits?

Maybe you always wanted to perform in a community theater. You loved plays in high school and always loved going to see performances, and now you have the time to engage in the theater yourself. Maybe you like the outdoors. You always enjoyed it when you had the time on vacation for a hike or visiting a national park. And now you can visit some of the great national parks across America. Maybe you always wanted to learn how to fly. The idea of piloting your own plane has excited you since you were young. Now is the time. It is your turn to spend time doing what you have dreamed of for years.

Plant a garden, build furniture, raise animals, train for a marathon, learn to sail, write a book—the list is endless. Any of these pursuits and many more can easily bring you years of fun and fulfillment. You can follow your passion and not feel guilty about it because this is your chosen retirement style.

Travel

Another traditional retirement style is travel. Many enter retirement with a Dream List (not a "bucket list" with its connotation of "before I kick the bucket," as if death should be the focus of a positive list). A Dream List includes countries to visit and experiences to have in special locations around the world. The choices in world travel are almost endless. Because of the massive number of retiring boomers (remember, 10,000 every day), the travel industry has responded with an impressive amount of options.

If you like traveling in groups, there are companies that do all the work for you. All you have to do is show up at the right place at the right time and off you go with everything taken care of for you. If you are more independent and adventurous, you can plan your own trips. Dealing with potential surprises or glitches is possible but researching and planning gives you control over what you see and do on your trip. This requires a large investment of time and energy, but it does give you the best opportunity to experience a given place or culture.

Cruising is one group travel option. Taking a cruise is a laid back, relaxing, almost serene way of traveling. You have the fresh sea air and exotic ports of call waiting to be explored. But you have all the comforts of home on the boat, and you can visit many places without ever checking in to a new hotel or repacking your luggage.

There are many cruise options available to you in the Atlantic, Pacific, Caribbean, Mediterranean, and Baltic regions. You could travel the great rivers of the world: the Rhine, Danube, Nile, Yangtze, or Mississippi. In fact, some people are choosing to embark on long-haul cruises permanently. Mario Salcedo has been living aboard cruise ships for twenty years. He said, "I decided I had enough of the corporate world and I wanted to spend the rest of my life traveling the world." (Verde 2017)

It may seem like this option is only practical for the super wealthy. But the *Journal of the American Geriatrics Society* did a study and concluded that spending twenty years (after age sixty-five) aboard a cruise ship would only cost a little over $2,000 more than the cost of living in a retirement home. (Verde 2017) The cruise ship lines have taken notice. Oceania Cruises has introduced "Snowbird in Residence" Caribbean voyages for up to 116 days. Crystal Cruises will introduce three vessels in 2022 that will include forty-eight privately leased "Crystal Residence" apartments.

You may be a true adventurer and want to go where everyone else does not. You can travel to exotic places only reached by small planes, camels, elephants, or by foot. These trips are far from relaxing, they are physically taxing and not for the faint of heart.

If you want to learn while traveling, there are literally thousands of educational tours and programs in many countries and all fifty states. These programs combine the best of learning and travel. You can directly experience the culture, history, art, and music you are learning about. I have had the opportunity to travel to six continents and see many of the great places in the world like the Sydney Opera House, Iguazu Falls, the Vatican, and many more. Travel is certainly an enticing style to consider.

Volunteer

The final traditional retirement style is the volunteer style. Volunteering has always been a popular choice for many people who retire. As the enormous boomer retirement movement continues, volunteering will evolve to include more meaningful expressions. The days of sealing envelopes, answering phones, and cleaning up will expand to include other options that match retirees' interests and skills. As a pastor I know firsthand the value of volunteers. Though my church has a younger demographic, I look forward to the days when our folks will retire and give greater amounts of time to serving the church.

As volunteer opportunities expand, there is a strong possibility that there will be one that aligns with your interests. But this new paradigm requires a higher degree of effort, energy, and discernment previously reserved for job hunting. The effort is worth it to both you and the nonprofit, a both will benefit from the relationship. The volunteer style is not just about volunteering but doing work that is genuinely gratifying. Volunteering will become more like employment that has intrinsic value rather than financial value.

I have seen firsthand the positive impact of volunteering. In my church there are hundreds of volunteers who help provide myriad ministries each week. Multiple Sunday services require another level of serving, especially when the services are contemporary and involve a band, sound, lights, cameras, and a studio. This is on top of the typical greeters, ushers, and children's volunteers needed in any church. For some of our church volunteers who have fit volunteering in around their demanding careers, the possibility of spending more time serving in retirement will be so rewarding because the stress and responsibility of their full-time job will finally be eliminated.

The UCLA Medical Center did a study of volunteers and found there is a host of positive benefits associated with volunteering. Physical benefits include living longer and having a stronger immune system and greater cardiovascular health. There are emotional benefits too, including increased self-esteem, less self-absorption, and a greater sense of control. And there are spiritual benefits, including feeling closer to God, having purpose in life, and having a sense of gratitude.

Beyond these empirical benefits, volunteering sets a positive example for others. It helps individuals appreciate the many blessings they have. It can give a true sense of meaning to your retirement years. You can use your unique skills and experiences in meaningful ways. And it allows you to meet new people and develop strong relationships. This style provides the opportunity for an impactful legacy.

Work

One of the new, modern styles of retirement is the work style. This seems like an oxymoron since we are retiring from "work," but the work will be different than the work we did throughout our careers. It may involve working for others or for yourself, using new skills or old ones, part-time or full-time employment, or maybe even doing work as part of the gig economy (short-term contracts or freelance work as opposed to permanent jobs).

There is much to determine about the work. What kind of work, how long we will work each day, what the salary is, and how many years we will perform the job. There are many paths you can take. Certainly standard employment in a small or large company, either full- or part-time, is one way to go. But much has changed regarding employment that you can take advantage of to find new appealing work.

The 77 million Boomers who retire will be replaced by only 48 million Gen Xers. Simple math tells us that work will be available. Certain sectors of employment are likely to be filled by retirees. Seasonal work, part-time work, and even work sharing are all much more suited to a retiree's schedule. More short-term, project-based work is being outsourced by companies. A majority of companies now use contract work on a regular basis, creating whole new employment opportunities. One of my retired pastor friends now does contract work for churches. When a church is in transition from one pastor to another, he works to guide the church through the process while keeping the ministry going strong during the transition.

The growth in online work that's done for clients without face-to-face communication and meetings taking place is booming. Work is brought to the worker instead of the worker being brought to the work. You gain the advantage of being able to work when and where you choose. One of my friends employs a virtual assistant. She does his clerical work, handles his schedule, and sets up his meetings. She functions like his executive assistant, but it is all done online. My friend saves money, and the virtual assistant has a great part-time job working from home.

Non-traditional contract workers now make up more than a third of the American workforce, and that number is growing at a rate double the traditional workforce (Florida 2014). Your ideal work may not have existed the last time you looked for a job. And your ideal work may be in a field you've never even heard of. The old either/or of work or retirement has been transformed. You may be finished with work that dominates your days, ties you down, and consumes your life. But you can now control the when and where of work, giving you the ability to work and have your freedom too.

Creative

Another modern style of retirement is the creative style. In your career you may or may not have been creative.

Research about the nature of work indicates that nearly 38 million Americans, some 30 percent of all employed people, create for a living. As a speaker and author, I have the joy of being a creative. Creating messages, articles, and books has allowed me to make a positive impact. The number of creatives has become larger than those in the working class, and they have an enormous influence over our culture.

We certainly value creativity in our culture. Classic creatives are those who create art and music, design fashion, or make movies and television. But now there is a larger group of creatives from the fields of business, healthcare, and law who create new products, technology, and services for our complex world. Whether an artist or an engineer, a musician or computer scientist, a fashion designer or app designer, what they all share a common creative ethic.

The creative style allows for self-expression, individuality, and openness to ideas. Instead of basing their value on whoever it is they work for, they base their identity on what they create. They value setting their own agenda, being themselves, and doing challenging work. They can work at any time because the creative switch cannot be turned on or off at predetermined times.

Creatives have a different sense of time. They will work for long periods of intense concentration, followed by complete breaks of activity dedicated to recharging or incubating ideas. They like to set their own hours, shape the content of their work, and express their identity through their work. The work environment is key and must be open to the free expression of ideas.

Whether you were a creative during your working years or not, this may be your retirement style. Do you have creative gifts? Are you a problem solver? Have you ever written or painted or composed music? Have you created new technologies, new services, or new content? Maybe you have, or maybe you could have but never had the opportunity. I know someone who loved to sing but never pursued it beyond singing in church. When he retired, he was able to start singing at various events and has found great joy in doing it.

You may have thought creative work was simply too impractical and pursued another career. But in retirement, you can now choose a style that will suit you and possibly stretch you in exciting new ways. Your latent gifts can now arise and extend blessings to you and others as well.

Entrepreneur

The entrepreneur style is certainly a modern style of retirement. Entrepreneurs find a need and meet the need, most often for profit but not always. Twenty-four years ago, I started a church to meet the needs of a younger generation that had given up on church or never went. We have had an amazing impact, reaching thousands of people locally and hundreds of thousands globally through our Internet Campus. Along the way, people have come to know purpose and meaning in their lives. They have connected with God in a personal way that has changed them and those they love.

There are many needs in our world, both existing and emerging, that can be met through an organization or business. They can have a definitive impact on the health and happiness of many people, including the well-being of people, animals, and our environment. The goal is to use our values to contribute something worthwhile to individuals and society. Boomers are well-positioned to create such organizations and businesses. They bring a wealth of experience, considerable assets, and an ability to communicate. This style may be exactly what you envision for your retirement.

Older Americans are leading the way in new business formation. According to the Ewing Marion Kauffman Foundation, the highest rate of entrepreneurship activity is among fifty-five to sixty-four-year-olds. Of those involved in early stage entrepreneurial activities, 18 percent are over fifty-five and 9 percent are over sixty-five. And *US News & World Report* notes that older owners are more successful, at least as measured by business survival rates (Moeller 2010).

Boomers came of age in the '60's and '70's and have a decidedly idealistic view as a generation. They thought they knew what needed to be changed. Whether some of what they changed (sexual revolution, material focus, entitlement mentality) is actually good will be judged by history. But many may still believe they know better than anyone else how to make the world a better place.

Is this the ideal style for your retirement? It is important to define terms. Many may think of entrepreneurship as starting a new business, but it is much more. In *Forbes* magazine, Candida Brush defines entrepreneurship this way:(Brush 2012) "It is a set of actions—it is identifying or creating an opportunity, marshaling the resources and providing the leadership and building a team to create something of value, either social or economic."

Have you ever identified a possibility or an opportunity to explore or create? When you focus on possibilities you will have more opportunities. Do you have a unique way to solve a nagging problem? Problem-solvers are definitely needed in our world. Would you enjoy taking your ideas to the next level? If you have a great new idea, that is where to start. To move forward is to adopt an entrepreneurial style.

Student

The final modern retirement style is the student style. Learning is good for the mind, but just because you once graduated and got a diploma or a degree doesn't mean you have to be done learning. If you have the student style, you can grow and develop and live out your full God-given potential. Study does not end when you finish going to school, it just changes. It may be a different kind of study, but it is still learning. Proverbs 1:5 tells us, "Let the wise listen and add to their learning, and let the discerning get guidance."

Studies can be a means to an end or the end in and of themselves. There are enormous options for what to study and to what degree. The Internet has exploded the number of options you now have for learning. This is why this style is such a viable choice for retirees. You may choose to study for the pure joy of learning, become skilled in a new area, or be knowledgeable in something of interest. Whatever the motivation, the result will be the benefit of learning something new. And there is a real sense of accomplishment when your skills or knowledge increase.

The possibilities for learning are endless, which is why this style is so good for retirement. You can take a class at your local community college or one at a local church. You can go to One Day University events offered at colleges and learn about four subjects in one day. You can take many different courses at www.thegreatcourses.com, where experts teach on a variety of subjects through video or audio. You can even learn for free at www.Edx.org, where online courses are offered from the best universities in the world like Harvard, Cal Berkeley, and MIT. Not to mention the plethora of educational podcasts that are now offered.

Seminars and workshops offer another way to learn. You can attend them locally or take a trip and combine travel with learning. You can learn a new skill like painting or pottery. Maybe even learn about a new field like physics or neuroscience. This can be a great time to learn more about God. Self-renewal and self-improvement happen through learning. What an excellent way to spend your retirement.

Reading will always be a mainstay for learning. Thanks to Amazon.com, the search for reading material has never been easier. In a short amount of time you can find a book on almost any subject. As you read and absorb the subject, your knowledge will grow. You will develop and expand your knowledge and insight. You will exercise your mind as you practice the student style.

. . . . .

The University of Chicago did a survey about aging (Harms 2016). They discovered optimism about growing older increased steadily with age. Among people in their thirties, 46 percent described themselves as mostly or somewhat optimistic about aging. But the optimism jumped to 66 percent of people seventy and older. I think the increase in confidence comes from the options available in retirement. Choosing a style that suits you results in a happy retirement.

RETIREMENT STYLES INVENTORY

- For each statement, mark to what extent it is true of your life:

3=VERY

2=SOME

1=LITTLE

0=NOT AT ALL

- Put a number in the blank before each statement.

- Transfer the numbers you gave for each statement to the grid at the end of the inventory.

- Total each column. The highest number identifies your preferred retirement style; the next highest number, your secondary style.

☐ 1. My retirement goal is to move to Florida, buy a house on a golf course, and enjoy rest and relaxation.

☐ 2. My "Dream List" includes visiting countries around the world.

☐ 3. When I retire I want to do something that is genuinely gratifying.

☐ 4. When I retire I would like to start a new "career."

☐ 5. I value setting my own agenda and doing challenging work.

☐ 6. I want to find a need and meet that need.

☐ 7. I believe retirement is not the time to stop learning.

☐ 8. I would like to pursue a hobby in retirement that I have not had time to do before.

☐ 9. I enjoy cruising because everything is taken care of for me.

☐ 10. I have too much energy to sit around. I want to form some great relationships that make a difference.

☐ 11. I want to continue to use the skills that I used during my career in retirement.

☐ 12. I like to set my own hours and express my identity through my work.

☐ 13. I want to have an impact on the health and happiness of many people.

☐ 14. I would like to become skilled in a new area in which I have interest.

☐ 15. I owned a small business and never had time for a vacation. I want to travel in my retirement.

☐ 16. I am a true adventurer and want to go where everyone else does not.

☐ 17. I want to set a positive example for others in my retirement.

☐ 18. I would like to perform special projects for different companies when I retire.

☐ 19. I am a problem solver and want to continue this into retirement.

☐ 20. I am really interested in starting a new business.

☐ 21. Self-improvement and self-renewal are very important in retirement

☐ 22. I don't see any need to have lunch with former colleagues or attend retirement parties. I just want to head off into the sunset.

☐ 23. I like to learn about other places: culture, history, art, and music.

☐ 24. I want to have a true sense of meaning in my retirement using my unique skills in meaningful ways.

☐ 25. In retirement I want to still make a difference for a company but be able to control when and where.

☐ 26. I like to work for long periods of time with intense concentration and then take a break to recharge.

☐ 27. I can create an opportunity, get the resources, provide leadership, and build a team to create something of value.

☐ 28. I want to develop and expand my knowledge and insight by exercising my mind.

Leisure	Travel	Volunteer	Work	Creative	Entrepreneur	Student
1.	2.	3.	4.	5.	6.	7.
8.	9.	10.	11.	12.	13.	14.
15.	16.	17.	18.	19.	20.	21
22.	23.	24.	25.	26.	27.	28.
Total	Total	Total	Total	Total	Total	Total

CHAPTER THIRTEEN

JESUS STYLE

O f all the great people who have lived throughout human history, there is arguably no one great- er than Jesus Christ. He founded the Christian faith that now numbers over two billion people. Good works done in his name have advanced virtually every human endeavor, from science to medicine to educa- tion. Even people who are not fond of organized religion see Jesus as someone to be admired.

And Jesus had a very particular style. He is unlike any- one who has ever lived on this earth. The way he lived his life and the incredible impact he had is unique in all of history. His compassion changed people, his leadership changed the world, and his resurrection changed eterni- ty. Let's look at the various styles of Jesus.

Shepherd

In John 10:11 Jesus said, "I am the good shepherd." Jesus had the shepherd style. It's a style that needs to be un- derstood because most of us don't know any shepherds or much about them. And it means God sees us as sheep, which is not a pretty picture. It is even somewhat insulting and offensive if you take it too personally. All the animals in the world and God chose sheep. He does not say we're like lions. He does not say we're like bears. He does not say we're like eagles. He says we're like sheep.

There have been sheep and shepherds since ancient times to the present day. The most famous king who ever lived was King David, and before he was a king, he was a shepherd. The first visitors to see Jesus were shepherds. There are 157 references to sheep in the Bible. Shepherds and sheep painted a picture everyone in ancient times could clearly understand. God chose this style as an easy way for us to understand who Jesus was and who we are.

What do we actually know about sheep? About the only thing most people know about sheep is that you can shear them to get wool. But there is so much more you need to know. Sheep require more care and attention than other livestock. And this is how God sees us. We are in need of extra attention.

Sheep are very fearful. For instance, if we're out in the woods and we're thirsty, most of us would look for running water. We'd like to get by a nice steady brook. If we see still or placid water, it's not as appealing to us. But sheep can get nervous around the sound of rushing water, so shepherds sometimes dam up the water to create a peaceful pool in order for them to drink. They have an unquenchable thirst and want to drink often but they can only drink when they're at peace. This is why the twenty-third Psalm says, "He leads me beside still waters."

Sheep are easily stressed. They will quickly panic and flee. They need a shepherd to help them be at peace and rest. Sheep have virtually no way to defend themselves. They have no claws or fangs, and they can't outrun most predators. Sheep simply cannot survive without a shepherd protecting them.

Sheep also have no sense of direction. They get lost easily. And white sheep are particularly vulnerable to predators because they can't blend into the environment. To make matters worse, they have horrible depth perception. They can only see about ten to fifteen yards in front of them. So they have no ability to defend themselves, get lost easily, and can hardly see what's in front of them.

But there's more. Sheep can fall over and they can't get up. Their short little stubby legs and their rather large bodies don't allow them to be able to get up. When they can't get up, gases build up inside their rumen and eventually cut off their circulation. If a sheep stays down and does not get rescued, the sheep will eventually die. They need a shepherd to get them back up.

Now there are a few good things about sheep. They have excellent hearing. What they lack in eyesight they make up for in hearing. They can hear their shepherd's voice from far away and recognize that it is his voice. Sheep have an amazing ability to remember a face for years. They can see a face, and even if some time passes, they will recognize the person if they see them again. Their memory is just that impressive. And of course, sheep do produce wool. Where would we be without wool to keep us warm?

Jesus is the good shepherd, but why is Jesus not the great shepherd? Why isn't he the greatest shepherd? Why is he just the good shepherd?" The word for "good" here in the Bible literally means "attractive" or "beautiful."

Used in this context, good implies "ideal" or "model." Jesus is the model shepherd. He is the ideal shepherd. He is the paradigm of all shepherds.

The shepherd is intimately involved with and aware of the needs of each of the sheep. He learns their different personalities, that some are stubborn, that some are hyperactive, and that some are melancholic. He understands they are different.

He protects the sheep because they are defenseless and can't protect themselves. In ancient times, shepherds protected their flocks from predators by using a rod, more like a club. If any animal tried to hurt, harm, or upset the sheep, the shepherd would take the club and use it against the predator. Ancient shepherds also used a staff, or a long pole with a crook on the end. They would put the crook around the neck of a stray sheep to gently guide them back to the path the rest of the flock was on.

Sometimes God has to bring things into our lives that are painful because he knows if we keep going down the path we're going it will end in disaster. A wolf will come when we're wandering one day and destroy us. He allows pain into our lives to draw us closer to him. He allows suffering in our lives that we might rely more on him.

Sheep need grass and water They need grass so much that if they can't find good pastures, they'll just start eating almost anything. They'll eat roots, dirt, and all kinds of stuff that isn't good for them. If they do not follow the shepherd into green pastures, they tend to go off and start eating in places that are not healthy for them. Places that do not bring them sustenance and the strength that they need, and can even poison them and make them sick.

We can be like sheep and inadvertently cause ourselves harm. We think we know what's best and choose not to trust God's timing. We move down our own paths instead of trusting His paths. But he's the good shepherd, and the welfare of the sheep are his primary focus. Every day the shepherd calls for the sheep. Likewise, Jesus calls to us through the Bible, which is why we have to read it, study it, and hear it preached. We can hear the shepherd's voice and we can respond to it.

Jesus is the model shepherd; he gave his life for us, his sheep. Jesus is the model of love, the model of giving, and the model of leading. The more we allow Him to guide us and lead us, the more provision, protection, and prosperity we'll have. Stay close to the shepherd—to Jesus—and your life will be infinitely better.

Teacher

Luke 10:25 says, "An expert in the law of Moses stood up and asked Jesus a question to see what he would say. 'Teacher,' he asked, 'what must I do to have eternal life?' " Everyone who encountered Jesus called him by the name of Teacher. Jesus's disciples called him Teacher. People seeking his help or advice called him Teacher. Even religious leaders opposed to Jesus acknowledged his teaching style. Even today, all major world religions acknowledge him as a teacher. Islam talks about Jesus as a prophet, someone who taught the words of God. Gandhi talked about Jesus and the remarkable nature of his teaching. Various Jewish scholars through the years, such as Samuel Ash and others, have recognized Jesus's teaching style.

For most of us, when we think of a teacher, what comes to mind is a school teacher who taught us or teaches our children. This was Jesus's role among his twelve disciples. The teacher style of Jesus includes education, but it is more expansive than that. Preaching was also a big part of Jesus's teacher style. He proclaimed God's truth. He was a public speaker who addressed large groups of people. In his public speaking, it was the nature of his teaching that made him unique and made his message powerful.

Jesus taught with authority. When people heard him speak, they said he spoke as one with authority. Why is that? It is because he spoke God's words, and listeners recognized it was different than just somebody talking or some other religious leader teaching. Jesus addressed needs and gave people answers. He showed how those needs could be met. He cared about what people thought, what they were going through, and how he could best reach them. This is why Jesus's teaching was so effective and why, all these years later, it's still guiding millions of people's lives.

Jesus is the model teacher. If you are a teacher, a speaker, or a preacher, you could never do better than to look at the model teacher Jesus. Effective teaching takes place anytime and anywhere. Anyone who understands communication knows this is true. Jesus was a master communicator. *Communicator* may be a better word than teacher to describe Jesus. He knew how to communicate in all kinds of settings. He wasn't limited to only speaking in a synagogue or to small groups. Jesus knew how to speak to any group at any time. He spoke to curious crowds, and he taught his committed core. In the Gospels, Jesus preaches on mountains, teaches in cities, and even speaks from a boat. Jesus would use any occasion to communicate his message.

Effective teaching always uses a variety of methods. People are diverse and hear in different ways. Jesus understood the need for variety. He would ask questions. In fact, Jesus asked 153 distinct questions in the Gospels. He would make comparisons. In the Sermon on the Mount (Matthew 5–7), he made 142 comparisons. Jesus used comparisons to help people understand big concepts. He would start with the known to help them understand the unknown. He would talk about having faith like a mustard seed, and they knew how small a mustard seed was. His listeners could immediately understand Jesus was saying they didn't need to have a huge amount of faith. They just had to have a little bit of faith.

Jesus spoke in parables, which are essentially short stories that use symbolism to illustrate a truth. In fact, about one third of all his speaking was done in parables. But he also used one-liners. Some of these lines are famous and significant to this day. He said, "You must be born again" (John 3:7 NIV). Of course that elicited a response. How can someone go and be born a second time? Jesus would also sometimes make shocking statements. He once said, "If anyone comes to me and does not hate father and mother, wife and children, brothers and sisters—yes, even their own life—such a person cannot be my disciple" (Luke 14:26 NIV). How strange it must have sounded to seemingly go against one of the Ten Commandments: "honor your father and mother" (Exodus 20:12 NIV).

He spoke this way because he was trying to engender a reaction. He was trying to get people's attention. Jesus used all these methods to communicate truth. Effective teaching relates truth to life. Jesus was the master of this, which is why he was such an incredible teacher.

In the Sermon on the Mount, an ideal model of Jesus's preaching/teaching, there is 35 percent content (what to know) and 65 percent application (how to put it into action). Jesus wanted his listeners to not just know what to do but how to do it. His teaching was full of ways to practically apply what they had learned.

Jesus established a point of contact with people. He found a way to take something that was familiar and use it as a way to teach. For instance, they were surrounded by vineyards so he would say he was the vine and they were the branches.

Jesus spoke a lot about agriculture. When you read his parables, you may notice he was always talking about the world in which he lived. This was an agrarian economy based on agriculture. He connected with people's common experiences. He talked about animals, about shepherds, about various crops. Jesus would also talk about water, because where Jesus lived, water was not plentiful and therefore it was very valuable. He talked about living water. As soon as Jesus said it, they knew exactly what he was talking about. Effective teaching ultimately always produces action on the part of the listener. It isn't just about sharing information. Jesus always made the application clear and understandable.

And his followers put his teachings into action. There is nothing in the world even close to the church of Jesus Christ in terms of members, impact, or influence. Jesus Christ proclaimed and taught a message, and 2,000 years later, it is the single biggest force in the world. Now that is effective teaching! Anyone would do well to follow someone who had that kind of production, success, and effectiveness.

This is just a partial list of his teachings: He taught about anger, anxiety, debt, and doubt. He taught about fasting, faith, giving, and greed. Also honesty, hypocrisy, joy, and knowledge. He taught about lust, marriage, parenthood, and prayer. Also respect, responsibility, sex, and stewardship. He taught about taxes, trust, wisdom, and zeal. Jesus taught about many life situations, occurrences and realities. He taught about life. The teachings of Jesus allow us to understand so much about all aspects of our lives. Though it is true Jesus didn't teach about everything, he taught principles that we can apply to any situation or life event. Jesus gave us a guide to living through his teaching style.

A person who builds their life upon the teachings of Jesus Christ will have a wonderful life, a marvelous life, a fantastic life. You cannot go wrong. They'll never guide or steer you in the wrong direction. You will never ever regret following Jesus's teachings. It is the best way you could ever live your life.

Friend

In John 15:15 Jesus said, "I don't speak to you as my servants. I speak to you as my friends." Jesus had the friend style. This is part of what makes Christianity unique—the idea that we could have a friendship with God, we could be friends with God. It is a unique concept. This is not found in Judaism, Islam, Buddhism, or Hinduism. No other belief system or world religion has this message of a personal relationship with God, that one could be a friend of God.

It is remarkable to think that we could be friends with God. Of course, it is contingent. Everyone is not automatically a friend of God. We can choose to be friends, just like any other friendship. We're not friends with everyone, but we can choose to enter into a friendship relationship with someone. We do need to understand what friendship means to Jesus and what it can mean for us.

Billy Martin, former New York Yankees ball player and manager, wrote *Number 1*, his autobiography. In it he shares a story about his teammate Mickey Mantle. Both Billy and Mickey loved to hunt. They were in Texas, and Mickey went to one of his buddies and asked if they could hunt on his ranch that day. His friend let them hunt but asked for a favor in return. His friend had a mule for many years that was now blind and needed to be put out of his misery. He did not have the heart to do it and wanted Mickey to do it for him. Since Mickey had his rifle for hunting, his friend wanted him to go into the barn and put the mule down, and Mickey agreed to do it.

When Mickey got back in the truck, he decided to have a little fun with his buddy Billy. He slammed the door and started cursing, saying, "This bum. He's supposed to be my friend and yet he's not going to let us hunt on his land today. I'm so mad at that guy that I'm going to go into his barn and shoot one of his mules." They drove the pickup up to the barn, and Mickey jumped out with his gun and shot the mule. Then just a few seconds later, Mickey heard two other gunshots. He ran back to the pickup and asked, "What just happened? What's going on?" Billy said, "I was so mad that guy would treat my friend like that, I took my gun and killed two of his cows" (Martin 1980).

It may be a bit misguided, but that is friendship. This is how friends are—they stick up for each other and are there for each other. Jesus Christ wants to be our friend. God entered the world for the purpose of opening the door to friendship.

We need to realize that Jesus's view of friendship is based on love. Jesus says, "I tell you to love each other, as I have loved you" (John 15:12). This is not a novel concept, but there is more to it. To properly understand the Christian faith and Jesus, you must recognize that it is Jesus who promotes the message of love. You're not forced into a relationship. You're invited into a relationship. The relationship is based on love, our love for Jesus, Jesus's love for us.

Jesus understands friendship as action. We have to do something. He initiates and we have to respond. Jesus said, "The greatest way to show love for friends is to die for them" (John 15:13). Jesus died on the cross for us, and in doing so, he demonstrated the greatest act of love.

Jesus recognizes friendship with him is based on communication. If there isn't communication, a friendship cannot develop. You can't develop a friendship if you don't communicate. He communicates with us through the Bible, the words of God to us, and we communicate with him through prayer.

And Jesus sees friendship evidenced by obedience. In John 15:14 he says, "You are my friends if you obey me." Love is not just about acceptance; it is also about obedience.

In John 15:14, *if* is the key word. It is a conditional word. "If you obey me, you are my friends." Our friendship with Jesus involves communication and action. It is based on love, and it requires our obedience. This is how Jesus defines friendship.

So, what can hinder a growing, deepening friendship with Jesus? How does that happen? One way we hinder our friendship is when we acknowledge Jesus and use him for our purposes, but avoid having a real relationship with him—saying things like, "I'm not into the church, I don't like religion, but I like Jesus, Jesus is cool."

Another way we can hinder friendship is by allowing our religious activities to become routine. Sometimes we actually do things that are religious in nature that ultimately end up taking us away from spending time with Jesus and getting to know him. For instance, the Apostles' Creed is recited in churches every Sunday, but some people are not really living (or believing) what the Apostles' Creed says. They're just saying it because it's the religious thing to do.

Going through the motions of giving can also adversely impact your relationship with Jesus—just giving God his part so nothing bad will happen to you financially. Going to church can hinder our friendship too if we think that giving God an hour on Sunday means the rest of the week is ours. By doing things that don't really develop your relationship with Jesus, you're just cloaking it in the guise of religious sincerity.

We can hinder our relationship with Jesus through busyness as well. We have to guard against being so busy that we don't have any time to spend with Jesus. I am a proponent of getting up earlier than necessary in the morning, when your mind is most clear, to spend time with Jesus before the busyness of the day takes over. What a great way to start your day. We have to watch out for busyness hindering our friendship. If we don't prioritize our schedule so our friendship with Jesus is first, we can get so busy that it gets pushed to the bottom of the list.

One more way our friendship with Jesus can be hindered is a lack of true communication. If your prayers are just a laundry list of needs, that is not two-way communication. "Jesus, do this stuff for me, amen." If the entire week goes by and you never pray, that is zero communication. Just try that with any relationship you have—the results won't be healthy. The other part of communication is listening. One way God talks is through the Bible. You can read it anytime you want, and God will speak to you through the words.

Servant

Matthew 20:28 (NIV) says, "The Son of Man did not come to be served, but to serve." Jesus had a servant style. Instead of using people, Jesus served people. His mission was to serve others and give his life away. He spent his time doing kind acts, relieving people's burdens, and bringing happiness. He taught his disciples about serving in many different settings, but he gave one very enlightening picture of serving.

He knew many may have a different picture of what a servant was like, so he showed a three-dimensional picture of what a servant really is. He wanted us to clearly understand serving. At the Last Supper, Jesus knew he was about to walk a road of great suffering. He was about to leave the earth, so he left us with a clear picture of serving.

Jesus knelt down in front of his disciples and washed their feet. This was the job of the lowliest of servants. In ancient times, people wore sandals on their feet or walked around barefoot. The walked on dirt roads that were littered with animal dung, garbage, and anything else that people threw away. To wash someone's feet meant encountering a whole lot of filth. It was a disgusting job that no one wanted to do.

Jesus served out of love, not duty. Many who serve in the military or as first responders do it out of a love of service. Some may do it for a job or even to get an education, but most do it out of a love for their community and country. The pay is not great, but they want to help people in need or protect people from danger. Duty is drudgery, but service with love is joy. Jesus shows us the picture of a servant who loves people and wants to serve them.

Some see serving negatively. They treat it like a duty and can become unsatisfied or even bitter. Service is sometimes hard, and people may let you down. But far more often it is good and life changing. When you serve with love, you get to be on the front lines of what God is doing. Serving with a heart of love can change this world one person at a time.

Imagine Jesus on that night. He knew the next day he would experience injustice. He knew he would be tortured. He knew he would be crucified on a cross and endure horrendous suffering. He could have thought of his own comfort. He could have asked the disciples to take care of him for that one night. But instead he served them and gave an example of service. In a moment of great stress, he chose to serve in a great way.

When Jesus bent down to wash the disciples' feet, he knew who he was and he knew who they were. In fact, they were arguing about which of them was the greatest and most important of the twelve. In the midst of all this, Jesus got a basin of water and a towel and began to wash the disciples' feet. Jesus taught them the greatness of service.

He even washed Judas's feet. He served the man who would later betray him. He was not giving up on Judas. It is easy to give up on people we don't agree with, who have different views or who don't do things the way we do. Jesus served anyway and we should too.

Jesus shows us that we serve imperfect people, and those imperfect people matter to him. Those people need His love and service. God may call you to serve people who aren't like you. They may have issues or problems, but they are no more imperfect than you are. They are worth your time and effort because they matter to him.

There was no spotlight on Jesus that night. He didn't look for acclaim or recognition. When we serve, no one may notice. Servants aren't showy. The Greek word in the Bible for servant means "to stoop down." Jesus illustrated serving by stooping down to lift others up. Humility is recognizing who we are and how great God is. We are to serve with a humble heart so God gets the attention and the glory.

Serving will always come down to meeting a need. The reality of this story is that the disciples' feet were dirty and needed to be cleaned. They were about to eat, and before they could do that, someone had to wash their feet. Jesus scrubbing their dirty feet is servanthood shown in a very practical way. No matter how important or great you think you are, no one is greater than Jesus. We are to serve as Jesus did, and servants meet people's needs.

Is God calling you to serve? Is there a need you can meet? Maybe you have been on the sidelines and it is time to get into the game. Look around and see where there might be a need for you to meet. Or see what others are doing and come along side of them to help. Serve like Jesus.

Savior

1 John 4:14 says, "God sent his Son to be the Savior of the world. We saw his Son and are now telling others about him." Jesus's ultimate style is Savior. Jesus came to this earth to save us. This is why he is the Savior. The reason he came to this earth is because we all need salvation. The idea of a savior presupposes that people need to be saved.

Maybe you think you don't need to be saved, you don't need to be rescued, you don't need any help. Yet, the Bible's message is that we are in need of salvation. All of us need to be saved because all of us are lost. We can't find our way to peace, purpose, or meaning. Jesus says in Luke 19:10 (NIV), "The Son of Man came to seek and to save the lost."

Maybe you don't think you are lost, that you are doing okay. You may not have all the answers, but you're doing alright, so why would you need saving? Or you may believe you don't need to be saved, that you will live your life the way you want to live it and whatever happens, happens.

Romans 3:23 says, "All of us have sinned and fallen short of God's glory." This means there's no one whose life is acceptable to God, who is perfect like God is. All of us have a terminal illness called sin. And we need to be saved. Another way the word *saved* can be translated is "healed." We are healed from our terminal illness. We are spared. Our lives are saved. If you still need convincing, just ask yourself, "Am I perfect?"

You may be a good person—maybe even a lot better than most people. But there's no person with any degree of intellectual or moral integrity who can say, "I am perfect." No one can say that, which means all of us have the same terminal disease of sinfulness. We do things we shouldn't. We say things we shouldn't. We fail to do things we should. We fail to say things we should. In the end, all have sinned and fall short of God's standard of perfection, which is why everyone needs a savior—everyone.

Romans 6:23 says, "Sin pays off with death. But God's gift is eternal life." The death this verse is referring to is not just a physical death but an eternal death. It is an eternal separation from God. Sin ultimately leads to separation from God, but God's gift is eternal life. God gave us the greatest gift, Jesus. God's gift is a Savior, and we all need salvation—otherwise, we are on a direct path toward both physical and eternal death. God looks at this world, and his standard of perfection is not met. God's justice has to be appeased, and Jesus is the one who provides it. He took the punishment for sin on the cross. He paid the price so we can be saved.

Jesus accepted the punishment for our sins. He received the discipline. God's justice demands punishment. Our legal system functions in the same way: Justice demands punishment when crimes are committed, when there is injustice and people break the law. Sin is the breaking of God's law. When we sin, there has to be punishment. This is why we all need salvation and Jesus is the Savior, because Jesus took the punishment for us. He took the punishment by going to the cross.

Jesus offers his perfection to God as the sacrifice for all the imperfect human beings that have lived, are living, and will live in the future. His sacrifice reconciles the broken relationship between God and humanity. The relationship continues to be broken until it is healed, until it is redeemed, until it is restored by our receiving what Jesus has done. His work has already been accomplished. That is a 2,000-year-old finality.

Jesus changes the relationship between a holy and perfect God and an unholy, imperfect human race. The enmity that exists is replaced with friendship. Jesus is the Savior. He changes the nature of the relationship. It's not because of anything that we do—we are saved by grace.

Christ makes us acceptable to God. Jesus offers his grace and forgiveness to any person who would simply accept it. We are saved when we accept Jesus Christ into our lives. Ephesians 2:8 says, "You were saved by faith in God who treats us much better than we deserve. This is God's gift to you and not anything you've done on your own." You are saved when you confess Jesus as Lord and believe in your heart that he rose from the dead.

We are saved from our sins by accepting Jesus, by having faith in Jesus, by believing in Jesus's perfect life, his virgin birth, his perfect, sinless life, his death on the cross, and his resurrection victory. When we confess that, when we agree with that, when we say that is true, then we are saved. Any person, whether young or old, male or female, of any race or ethnicity—anyone can be saved.

There is a powerful story about a daughter and a mother from Brazil. The daughter was named Christina. The mother was named Maria. Maria's husband died, leaving her and her young daughter alone. They had a very difficult life. Maria made just enough money to get by. Christina didn't like the small village, and she longed to go to the big city where she thought she would be able to have what she could never afford in the village. She told her mother about her dreams, and Maria cautioned her that jobs were scarce and life could be difficult.

Christina had no skills and no way of making money. One morning Maria woke up to find that her daughter was gone. She knew that she had left and gone to the city. Maria gathered up her belongings, took whatever money she had, and headed for the bus station. But before she went to the bus station, she stopped by the drugstore. She went into a little photo booth and spent all this money taking pictures of herself. She got her pictures, headed on the bus, and went into the city.

She decided to frequent places she thought her daughter might end up going out of desperation. When you run out of money and you're hungry, you'll do things you never thought you would do. She went to places like bars, hotels, and nightclubs.

Wherever she went, she took one of the pictures of herself and tape it on a mirror in a bathroom or on a bulletin board at a hotel. She would put the picture anywhere she thought it would be seen. She searched for days for her daughter, putting up these pictures everywhere she went. She kept asking about her, but no one knew anything.

Finally, Maria had no more money. She had to go back home. Brokenhearted, she got back on the bus and headed back for the village she lived in. Several weeks later, Christina was walking down the stairs of a hotel. She wasn't the jubilant, excited young lady she had been. She was tired, disillusioned, and broken. The city life she had dreamed of had become a nightmare.

As she was reaching the bottom of the stairs, she noticed a small picture on a bulletin board. She immediately recognized the picture. Her throat tightened, her eyes began to tear up. She went over and took the picture off the board. She turned the picture over and written on the back were these words: "Whatever you've done, whatever you've become, it doesn't matter. Please come home. Love, Mom." And that very day she went home.

This is the story of Jesus the Savior. He's been putting his picture all over the place. Everywhere you go in your life. His message to you is, "Come home. Stop trying to do what you can't do in your own strength and your own ability. Stop going down all these roads that will never lead to happiness and peace. Come home." Jesus's arms are always extended. Statue after statue of Jesus depicts his arms extended. Jesus is saying, "Come home." It doesn't matter what you've done. It doesn't matter what you've become. Just come home. The Savior welcomes anyone who would respond to his invitation.

Pray this prayer right now: Jesus, I accept you into my life today. I confess all my past sins, mistakes, and failures. I ask you to forgive me. I believe that you are the

Savior. I ask you to be my Savior. Come into my life today and guide me and direct me in the plan you have for my life. In your name, Jesus, amen.

NOTES

Belk, Russell. Vol. 3, No. 3, December 1976. "It's The Thought That Counts: A Signed Digraph of Gift-Giving." *Journal of Consumer Research.*

Biehl, Bobb. 2005. *Team Profile.* The Masterplanning Group.

Brush, Candida. June 10, 2012. "Are You an Entrepeneur?," *Forbes.*

Duckworth, Carolee, and Marie Langworthy. 2013. *Shifting Gears To Your Life & Work After Retirement.* New Cabady Press.

Florida, Richard. 2014. *The Rise of the Creative Class.* New York, NY: Basic Books.

Goleman, Daniel. March/April 2000. "Leadership That Gets Results," *Harvard Business Review.*

Harms, William. May 16, 2016. "Overall Health Predicts Mortality Better Than Age, Study Finds," *UChicago News,* https://news.uchicago.edu/story/overall-health-predicts-mortality-better-age-study-finds

Hawkins Adams, Stacey. February 28, 2016. "Taking Back The Reins of Authority as Parents," *Richmond Times-Dispatch.*

Heimlich, Russell. December 29, 2010. "Baby Boomers Retire." *Pew Research Center*

Hybels, Bill, and Mark Mittelberg. 1994. *Becoming A Contagious Christian.* Grand Rapids, MI: Zondervan.

Kanner, Bernice. 1995. *Are You Normal.* New York, NY: St. Martin's Paperbacks.

Kosslyn, Stephen M., and G. Wayne Miller. 2013. *Top Brain, Bottom Brain: Surprising Insights Into How You Think.* New York: Simon & Schuster.

LeFever, Marlene D. 1995. *Learning Styles: Reaching Everyone God Gave You.* Colorado Springs, CO: Cook Communications Ministries.

Lythcott-Haims, Julie. June 30, 2015. A Former Stanford Dean On The Danger of Overparenting By Parents And Startups. *TechCrunch.*

Martin, Billy. 1980. *Number 1.*New York, NY: Delacorte Press

McCarthy, Bernice. 1987. *The 4MAT System: Teaching To Learning Styles With Right/Left Mode Techniques,* Barrington, IL, Excel Inc, 1987.

Moeller, Phillip. October 2010. *US News & World Report*.

Parrott, Les. November/December 2006. What Time Style Is It? *Rev! Magazine*.

Rath, Tom. 2007. *StrengthsFinder* 2.0, New York, NY: Gallup Press.

Sullivan, Robert. January 1994. Roper/Starch Worldwide Money Survey. *Worth Magazine*.

Thomas, Gary. 1996. *Sacred Pathways*. Grand Rapids, MI: Zondervan.

Verde, Tom. March 26, 2017. A Floating Retirement. *New York Times*.

Willyerd, Karie. December 23, 2013. Parents May Be Your Secret Weapon For Recruiting and Retaining Millennials. *Harvard Business Review*.

Zagorsky, Jay. Volume 35, Issue 5, September–October 2007, Pages 489-501. Do You Have To Be Smart To Be Rich? *Intelligence*.